SIGNS,
WONDERS,
& BEYOND

SIGNS, WONDERS, & BEYOND

Personal Testimonies from the Mission Field

IPE MATHAI

This is a publication of:

Mathai Outreach Ministries
P.O. Box 96495, Houston, Texas 77213-6495
Email:info@mathaioutreach.com

Website: www.mathaioutreach.com

Trilogy Christian Publishers

A Wholly Owned Subsidiary of Trinity Broadcasting Network

2442 Michelle Drive

Tustin, CA 92780

For information, address Trilogy Christian Publishing

Rights Department, 2442 Michelle Drive, Tustin, CA 92780.

Trilogy Christian Publishing/ TBN and colophon are trademarks of Trinity Broadcasting Network.

For information about special discounts for bulk purchases, please contact Trilogy Christian Publishing.

Trilogy Disclaimer: The views and content expressed in this book are those of the author and may not necessarily reflect the views and doctrine of Trilogy Christian Publishing or the Trinity Broadcasting Network.

10 9 8 7 6 5 4 3 2 1

Library of Congress Cataloging-in-Publication Data is available.

ISBN 979-8-89333-019-9

ISBN 979-8-89333-020-5

DEDICATION

This book is dedicated to the co-laborers, partners, and well-wishers of the ministry.

FOREWORD

It is with deep gratitude and great joy that I am writing a few words for my brother Ipe Mathai's new book, *Signs, Wonders, and Beyond.* As the title of the book suggests, it is a book on the supernatural works of God. It is an up close and personal look into Ipe's experiences, especially his mission work through Mathai Outreach Ministries. It is a follow-up book to Ipe's autobiographical work, *A Handful of Clay in the Potter's Hand*, which was published in half a dozen languages and thousands of copies, and which are being distributed far and wide.

Signs, Wonders, and Beyond is a compendium of many out-of-the-ordinary events Ipe and his ministry team have encountered in the course of his mission work in India, mainly in the states of Kerala, Tamil Nadu, Maharashtra, and Orissa. The twenty-nine chapters in the book are twenty-nine stories representing the many events and experiences that have transpired in the ministry's work since the publication of the first book. Over the last twenty years, many healings, deliverances from evil spirits, supernatural protection and provisions of God, outreach in unreachable areas, planting of churches, orphanages, schools, and much more have been a part of the mission and purpose of the ministry. The miracles of "Monsoon Stopped in Wynand" and the profuse rain that ended "The Drought in Jalna" are of Biblical proportions. Even the hundreds of baptisms are a miracle in and of themselves. On the whole, it is a testimony of God's power made manifest by the operation of the Holy Spirit and in the mighty name of Jesus!

Speaking of the preeminence of Christ in His ability to save, Hebrews 3: 4–5 says, *"How shall we escape if we* neglect so great a salvation, which at the first began to be spoken by the Lord, and was confirmed to us by those who heard Him, God also bearing witness both with signs and wonders, with various miracles, and gifts of the Holy Spirit, according to His own will." The Geneva Study Bible elucidates this passage with this explanation: "This is the true purpose of miracles. Now they are called signs, because they appear as one thing, and represent another: and they are called wonders, because they represent some strange and unaccustomed thing: and powers because they give us a glimpse of God's mighty power."

I will conclude with three points to ponder: 1. The salvation we have received is precious and priceless, and therefore, we cannot ignore it. 2. Because it is so great and precious, we cannot but publish it at any cost. 3. The most effective way of "preaching" the gospel of salvation is with the support of signs, wonders, and miracles to prove its authority and reliability. I humbly pray that God Almighty bless the author of this book and prosper this noble effort to glorify His holy name! Amen!

Bishop Dr. Varghese L. Mathai, ThD., PhD.
Gospel Light Mission
Fort Lauderdale, Florida

My dear brother Ipe Mathai's new book, *Signs, Wonders, and Beyond* is packed with marvelous stories of God's saving, healing, and life-transforming power. Over the years, his love for Jesus and his passion to serve the lost and hurting have been an inspiration for us all. This book is a remarkable account of the gospel's good news coming with life-changing, darkness-defeating power. Read it and let God take your faith to the next level!

Steve Young
Houston, Texas

Ipe Mathai's account of miracles and healings are great testimonies of what the Lord Jesus is still doing today and will forever be doing—using ordinary people and His authority. I salute him for writing *Signs, Wonders, and Beyond* because I, too, am a miracle. Given only a few weeks to live thirty-one years ago because of liver cancer, I know for a fact that miracles are real. Be blessed, helped, and filled with hope as you read this book.

Dodie Osteen
Co-Founder of Lakewood Church/Author of Healed of Cancer
Houston, Texas

This book is a testimony of how God used Brother Ipe Mathai in touching thousands of lives and helping establish His heavenly Kingdom with His love and miracle working power. I truly believe in all the testimonies written in this book, as I myself have experienced such supernatural miracles and testimonies during my trips to India and the ministry areas of Mathai Outreach Ministries. God is doing amazing things among the people in India and we are blessed to be participating and experiencing His miracle working power. Brother Ipe is a great influence and encouragement for me, especially to be committed in ministry.

Isaac Easow
Houston, Texas

CONTENTS

INTRODUCTION 13

HEALINGS AND MIRACLES 15

1.Deliverance from the Bondage of Smoking. 19

2.Healing of the Blinded Eye 27

3.Armugham's Story—Healing by Jesus' Touch . . .37

4.A Twin Sister Dying of Kidney Disease 45

5.A Woman with Kidney Tumors Healed. 51

6.An Inoperable Thyroid Tumor Healed. 55

7.An AIDS Patient Healed 61

8.A Healing Story in Rahuri 65

9.Healing of Sickle Cell Anemia 69

10.Healing of Severe Asthma 73

HEALINGS AND BAPTISMS. 75

11.Healing of Congenital Heart Disease. 77

12.Epilepsy Healed after Baptism. 79

13.Simon the Mental Patient Gets Healed 81

14.Postpartum Psychosis Healed 85

15.The Spirit of Fear Cast Out 89

16.Set Free from Religious Bondage 93

17.Infertility Healed 97

HEALINGS AND DEMON POSSESSION 101

18.A Man with Kidney Disease Healed 105

19.Girl with Chronic Headaches Delivered
   from Demonic Possession 109

20.The Suicidal Man Set Free. 115

21.A Blind Woman Healed 119

22.Delivered from Alcoholism and Suicide 123

SIGNS AND WONDERS 125

23.Breaking the Chain of Poverty 127

24.A Criminal Becomes an Evangelist 131

25.Story of My Last Rupee. 135

26.Out of Body Experience. 137

27.Escape from Naxalite Guerillas 139

28.The Monsoon Stopped in Wayanad 141

29.The Drought in Jalna 143

30.30-Day Government Department Shutdown . . .147

WHAT IS BEYOND? 149

An Invitation. 153

About Mathai Outreach Ministries 155

INTRODUCTION

In this book, *Signs, Wonders and Beyond,* my father writes a culmination of stories that reveal the power of our true and living God. Now more than ever, the world is in need of supernatural intervention as creation longs for the redemption of our Savior, Jesus Christ. More so, even in our own personal lives we seek God for His redemptive touch in our relationships, health, finances, and future and we look for the finished work of the Cross available to us, but we find that in order to see our miracle, we must have one thing—belief.

The following excerpt from John 4 talks about Jesus performing His second sign after coming from Judea to Galilee.

> *Once more he visited Cana in Galilee, where he had turned the water into wine. And there was a certain royal official whose son lay sick at Capernaum. When this man heard that Jesus had arrived in Galilee from Judea, he went to him and begged him to come and heal his son, who was close to death. "Unless you people see signs and wonders," Jesus told him, "you will never believe." The royal official said, "Sir, come down before my child dies." "Go," Jesus replied, "your son will live."*
>
> *The man took Jesus at his word and departed. While he was still on the way, his servants met him with the news that his boy was living. When he inquired as to the time when his son got better, they said to him, "Yesterday, at one in the afternoon, the fever left him." Then the father realized that this was the exact time at which Jesus had said to him, "Your son will live." So he and his whole household believed.*

As I read this passage, I think about how Jesus told the royal official that it would take signs and wonders for him to truly believe. I imagine the desperation of the father wanting his son to live when he begged Jesus to come and heal his son. I also took notice that Jesus never went to the boy; He simply said, "Go, your son will live." Lastly, these words from the chapter leapt out to me: "the man took Jesus at His word."

This royal official heard about what Jesus could do but did not fully know. His desperation took him to Jesus, and Jesus was ready to meet him at the point of his belief. All it took was one man's faith to see the signs and wonders Jesus promised he would receive. He took Jesus at His word.

As you read the stories from my father in this book, they are an account of the signs, wonders, and miracles of individuals that took Jesus at His word on the mission field where my parents were sent to serve in India and around the world. But before my father could "go," he was like that man who was desperate for an encounter with a miracle-working God. And God met him at the point of his belief, performing miracle after miracle in his own life through various signs and wonders. The hope is that you will read these stories, recognize the power of God that is available in your own life, and take Jesus at His word. He is ready to perform miracles in your life as He promised—just believe.

Sarah Moses, LMSW

HEALINGS
AND MIRACLES

"God also testified to it by signs, wonders and various miracles, and by gifts of the Holy Spirit distributed according to his will" (Hebrews 2:4).

Healing and miracles are the gifts of the Holy Spirit and are testimonies of how God demonstrates salvation through Jesus Christ. Miraculous healings are supernatural events that God performs through His servants. There are scores of healings written in biblical scriptures that testify to this. The Gospels have recorded several miracles and healings by Jesus Christ, and the book of Acts has records of many miracles and healings by the apostles in the early church. For centuries since, God has appointed prophets and His anointed servants through whom He performs similar and even greater healings and miracles across the world, even until this day.

"Very truly I tell you, whoever believes in me will do the works I have been doing and they will do even greater things than these, because I am going to the Father" (John 14:12).

In the following stories you will read a few of these supernatural testimonies of deliverance, healings and miracles that are beyond human understanding, just as it is written in God's Word.

Though I live in America, I travel to various countries as a missionary, a tourist, or as a businessman. On my way to India, I often stopped in other countries and met friends, relatives, random strangers, and acquaintances, besides many others who I met through my work with various organizations. I have always tried my best to use these opportunities to be a witness to share the gospel and pray for those in need or in a crisis.

From my early days of faith in Jesus Christ, I have experienced many miracles and supernatural healings in my personal life. When I was saved, baptized by the Holy Spirit, and transformed, God anointed me with the gift of healing and gave me power and authority over demonic spirits.

After the Lord called me in 1993 to go back to my people and be used as His vessel, my wife and I spent an average of two to three months per year in India doing mission work. Our goal then and now has been to share the gospel, the love and power of God. We talk about what the Lord has done in our lives, as well as share stories like the ones that follow. Whether in a hotel lobby or airport, in a Hindu, Buddhist or Islamic nation or to an atheist, in remote villages or urban towns, I share the truth of what I have seen and experienced. These stories resonate with them, because no matter the culture, language, or religion, the stories of pain and suffering are all similar. In my professional life in India and then America, I have worked in healthcare, which also allowed me to see the difference between medical cure and supernatural healings. I realized that a life full of joy and peace with God is only possible when one has experienced His supernatural deliverance and healing, which I can testify to. I am so honored that God has called me to be a minister of the Gospel of Jesus Christ because it lets me share the love and power of God with others and see life-transforming miracles take place in people from all walks, faith, and beliefs.

Our ministry began in the early 1990s in the town of Pandalam, which was also my hometown in the south-central region of the state of Kerala in South India. For many years, our senior pastor, Peter John, and I worked together and saw many deliverances and healings in the region. Then we moved to

Wynand in northern Kerala, where many of my close family and relatives are settled. Thereafter, we focused on the neighboring southern state of Tamil Nadu and then moved on to the western state of Maharashtra. Today, Mathai Outreach Ministries is doing ministry work in eleven states in India—South, West, East, and North. These are the places you will read about in this book, places where the miracle working power of God was manifested and continues to change and transform lives across the nation.

On the following pages, I am sharing a few of my experiences from our missions. In each story, the Lord guided me for His purpose to these people and circumstances. Some of the events you will read about may seem strange or unbelievable, but I want to share them with you because they are the facts and realities of our ministry. For those that have a desire to be a missionary, we want to prepare you for the ministry God has called you to, by letting you see how the supernatural power of God worked through our ministry. Let all glory and honor be unto Him forever and ever!

1.
DELIVERANCE FROM THE BONDAGE OF SMOKING

When I was nine years old and in middle school, one day I was helping my grandmother in the kitchen of my childhood home in Pandalam. Accidentally, a pot of boiling oil caught fire and large flames started leaping from the stove together with the burning oil. When I started screaming, my father came rushing in to help. He took the boiling pot of oil and started moving away from the fire; however, while doing that, the boiling hot oil spilled and splashed onto me as I was nearby. The oil splashed on my face, forehead, and many parts of my body.

A local physician came to our home and treated my burns. But the blisters from this fire accident left deep scars on my forehead and eyebrows that I had to live with throughout my childhood and youth.

I could in no way hide these scars, so I had to walk around with a lot of low self-esteem. I had to face the kids at school who would sometimes laugh and make fun of it or be critical. I then started withdrawing and isolating myself from my regular school friends. However, I started making friends with some of the grownups, the workers who did some labor work for my father. These were of a lower class and very simple-minded people, and I felt comfortable among them and didn't have to be embarrassed.

While mingling with these laborers, I picked up their habits and soon started learning how to smoke with handmade cigarettes, locally known as "beedi," made of leaves with some tobacco. Then later, I started using regular cigarettes. This smoking habit gave me a lot of pleasure and companionship, making me feel good, as this was an escape from the thoughts of low self-esteem. I now became a habitual smoker even before I turned into a teenager. I used to hide this habit from my parents and others who knew our family, smoking whenever possible.

This addiction to smoking also caused me to run away from home when I was in middle school. I ran far away from home, like almost four hundred miles away in the neighboring state of Karnataka, to a distant relative who was also a smoker and accepted me even though I smoked as a little kid. I stayed there for over two months. But my family found out where I was and took me back home. I resumed attending my middle school and eventually graduated.

Moving on to high school, I had more liberty to smoke. The kids and schoolteachers were from areas outside of our home area community, so not immediately known to my parents and neighbors. I now had more friends and together we used to even cut classes and go enjoy smoking. This addictive habit had now become an essential part of my everyday life.

I used to get money from my parents by lying to them about some other needs, but then used the money to buy smokes. So this habit caused me to start lying and even stealing from home frequently. I also stole crops like coconuts, mangoes, bananas, and black pepper from my father's field and traded them to get money for cigarettes or dining out with friends. 'I was no longer worried about being seen smoking in public.

However, my parents eventually came to know. Sadly, it also brought embarrassment and disrepute for my father, who was a well-respected schoolteacher in our town. Smoking was considered taboo in our society, especially among the Christian community. I used to then hide away from my father and avoid family dinners and prayer time just so that I was not confronted about it.

I was barely making my grades and didn't commit much time and attention to my studies. However, I graduated from high school and even joined the nearest college for a year.

During that year in college, I had no particular interest in studies, but I was actively participating in local politics. Those days there was some rebellion against the local state government, which was controlled by the communists. This was also the first communist government in any province of India. I joined local organizations that protested government functions and hampered public bus services, like picketing and causing road blockages.

I was an open rebel and living independently controlled by my self-indulgences and addiction to smoking. I was already planning to escape from my family and leave for some other place. I had some money that I got by selling our crop produce, and with this money I finally left home without my family's awareness.

I ended up on the streets of Mangalore in the neighboring state of Karnataka, just as when I ran away the first time. I started working at a local restaurant to support my basic needs. I was homeless and had no place to stay. So, I used to sleep at the nearby bus station on benches in the waiting area. However, I enjoyed my freedom to do whatever I felt like doing with no family, neighbors, or relatives to question me.

The thief came to steal my youth, innocence, and my purpose to live a normal childhood with traditional family values and upbringing. I spent a lot of my young days in rebellion.

The enemy wanted to destroy me, and it seemed that he was winning in his plan.

During my homeless days in Mangalore, I started training to be a typist. A colleague there helped me get connected to a hospital program at Father Muller's hospital in Kankanady, Mangalore. The program was conducted by the Swiss Emmaus association, and they had an opening for a trainee as a paramedic. I applied for that position and was accepted. That year was 1963. I completed the training program in nine months. After the training I was recruited by the Swiss Emmaus as a paramedic. I was among only the two out of a total of fifteen finalists who were recruited. I continued to work at the Swiss Emmaus for about six years. During this season I was a casual Christian, occasionally attending traditional church services with colleagues, but my heart was far from godly ways of living. I continued to smoke and hang out with secular colleagues and enjoyed their companionship.

In the mid-1960s, the chief medical officer was a Swiss trained plastic surgeon who led the Swiss Emmaus project. He trained me to assist him in the operation theater. One day, he noticed the big, deep scar on my forehead. After examining the scar, he assured me that he would operate to remove the scar tissue and make the skin on my forehead back to normal. He did an amazing "zigzag" procedure that eventually took the burn scar off, and I got my normal face back.

I was about twenty-six years old at the time of that plastic surgery. After having to live with that ugly-looking scar on my forehead and eyebrows for nearly sixteen years of my youth, this recovery was a great blessing and helped me regain some self-esteem because of my improved physical appearance. However, I continued to smoke, and my heart was still stubborn and hardened towards godly ways.

After working with them for about six years, Swiss Emmaus offered me the option to choose a career path and gain some additional professional training. I chose to pursue my career in professional nursing. I was sent to a three-year training course for nursing at the Salvation Army hospital located in Nagercoil, one of the southernmost towns of India, in the state of Tamil Nadu. This hospital was a very reputable institution in that region. Swiss Emmaus wanted me to work from their hospital located in the town of Hubli, to manage the nursing department that cared for leprosy patients. This training in nursing would qualify me for that role.

The hospital at Nagercoil was CBH (Catherine Booth Hospital), which is a Salvation Army hospital under the aegis of the Christian Medical Association of South India. The training institution had a strict Christian code of conduct and expected students and employees to follow Christian principles. There was strict monitoring by the warden, staff, and administrators. There was no room to practice any unhealthy habits or bad behavior, which could lead to immediate suspension or dismissal from the institution. When I left Mangalore, my ex-boss had warned me that "now you are on your own, and if for any reason you get into trouble with the institution management, we will not be able to influence their decision, as it is not in our control."

When I reached the institution, I had plenty of supplies of cigarettes with me at first. I used to keep it hidden from public view, trying to smoke as and when possible, but it was getting very difficult to keep practicing smoking, and I got very frustrated with the addictive need. I didn't want to be seen as a rebel in this institution and lose my opportunity to complete this course. I didn't want to face such embarrassment. But I just couldn't stay away from the smoking habit. This caused me great distress.

One of those early days at the institution, at the height of my distress, while I was resting in my dorm room by myself, I cried out to God to help me, asking Him to take away this habit of smoking from me once and for all. This was the first time I strongly felt the need to break away from this bondage and to plead with God for help.

The Lord heard my cry and delivered me from the craving to smoke, once and for all. So, after fourteen years of smoking addiction, this habit suddenly came to cease for good. On many earlier occasions, many people apart from my own family had kept advising me to quit and many times even rebuked or beat me for smoking. If I didn't get to smoke, I used to try other substances like chewing tobacco or sniffing snuff. So, this strong bondage had opened the door to all kinds of other rebellious habits.

However, after I cried out to God and renounced this addiction, I had no interest in taking a puff of any kind, nor did I want to pursue any of the other substance abuse habits I had developed through my youth. The Lord had truly delivered me from bondage to substance abuse.

When I was crying out to God to help me renounce, I was alone in the presence of the Lord, a lost sinner in a hopeless situation. I wasn't sitting in front of a pastor or a priest or a Christian counselor who would convict me of sin or present to me the gospel. I was deep in addiction, and I needed freedom. I had no clue about what salvation meant, the steps that led one to salvation, confessing a sinner's prayer or standing up in an altar call. I simply surrendered and humbled myself in the presence of the Lord. It was my own personal confession out of my own heart; my own simple sinner's prayer.

When I confessed my sinful addiction from the depths of my heart in repentance to turn away from this bondage, the Lord heard me. I experienced His forgiveness and His compassion, which comforted me at that time. I received His peace.

The deliverance from the bondage of smoking was the beginning of my acceptance of Jesus Christ as Lord and Savior in my life. He not only delivered me, but took away this huge burden of sin from my life.

These were my first meaningful steps in earnestly seeking the Lord and His purposes for my life.

2.
HEALING OF THE BLINDED EYE

I graduated from the nursing school in Nagercoil in the summer of 1971. I did well during my nursing course there. I was the top student in the first year, got a distinction in the second year, was elected the president of the student association in the third year and was the top student again. All of these made me feel confident and content, especially after my initial frustrations with smoking and after God delivered me from that bondage and I began my relationship with Him.

After I graduated from the nursing school in Nagercoil in July 1971, I left from there to go to Hubli, where I would start working in the new hospital for leprosy patients run by Swiss Emmaus. I decided to travel by bus all the way, a 650-mile journey. But en route, I stopped by and spent a couple of days with my parents. Then I boarded another bus to go on my onward journey. However, I decided to stop at the northern Kerala city of Calicut where my elder brother was working. I spent the night with him at his place. During my travels, I had started feeling some discomfort in my right eye. However, I left the next day as planned and boarded the bus to go onward to Hubli via the large city of Bangalore. During this bus journey, my eye started hurting worse, and I could see some dark spots and a shadow moving through the eye, preventing full vision.

I arrived in Dharwad (the town next to Hubli) where our temporary office was located and met with my boss. The next day, while having lunch with him, I told him about the discomfort and changes that were affecting my right eye during my journey. He was also a physician. He took me gently to the medical college hospital located in town. We met with the chief ophthalmologist for consultation. Upon examining my eye, he initially diagnosed that there was bleeding inside that eye. He advised me to take complete bed rest for one month and to come see him again. He didn't provide any specific medication since it was something internal in the eye. I was brought back to my residence. My boss assigned one of the assistants to care for me while I was resting. He was available twenty-four seven as needed. I somehow completed one month's bed rest. I couldn't do any work because I had to take a complete rest and was almost bedridden. I couldn't even get up out of bed without support. However, my eye situation got worse during that month.

I went back to the ophthalmologist after one month as directed, but after examining me he said there was no improvement, so he advised me to continue bed rest for another month. But during the second month, I started running a fever of 104–105° F. This fever didn't relent or drop off for several days and went on for long periods. I was admitted to Hubli Medical College Hospital in the ICU for further observation and treatment. I was getting weaker physically and also losing weight.

I was on the hospital bed with several diagnostic procedures being done on me. However, they couldn't find out what exactly was causing the fever. So they treated me for tuberculosis, took a liver biopsy to check for an abscess, and many other things. But the fever continued to stay and remain high.

One morning, the fourteenth day at the ICU, after my morning care, my attendant went to take care of my laundry. I don't remember whether I was in a coma or in a deep sleep, but suddenly I woke up when I heard a voice. But I didn't see anyone in my room; it was Jesus Christ speaking to me in a vision.

"Look around you and see who can help you now."

I immediately visualized my work colleagues, boss, attendant, my family, friends, and others whom I knew closely, all of those whom I had valued. But none of them were there to help me at that time of deep distress. My answer in my thoughts was "no-one!" I started weeping and wailing loudly. My situation was so helpless and hopeless. I had come all the way with great expectations for myself and the hospital management and now I was lying there helpless and unable to function normally or do any work, let alone take care of myself. After I cried out and wept, I felt a great peace and an assurance that I was now in the hands of Jesus.

My boss sent a telegram to my parents (those days there were no phones at our home or anywhere nearby) and asked them to come quickly. My father and my younger brother immediately started from home, arriving at the hospital two days later. My condition remained the same, and I stayed in the ICU. My father left to go back home after two days, but my younger brother remained there to care for me. After a few more days in the ICU, they were still unable to make any conclusive diagnosis. I then requested that I be discharged and sent back to my accommodation. My fever remained for another month. My brother was still with me and cared for my needs twenty-four seven. Meanwhile, I continued to deteriorate in my physical health, lost a lot of weight, and became like skin and bones, with long shabby hair and a long beard. I weighed about ninety-nine pounds.

My family and other believers back in my hometown were praying for my recovery.

One day we noticed that the fever came down to 99 degrees. This was the first time in two months that we saw the fever drop. That improvement continued for three days. Then my brother and I decided to leave and go home. After arriving at my Pandalam home, I continued to be sick and unwell, although the fever wasn't that high. I was very weak and barely able to stand up without assistance. But after several weeks, I could finally at least have a little of our family home cooked meal.

Leelamma, my younger sister, who is a very anointed spiritual prayer warrior, told me that they would be in fasting prayer the next day and had invited some special guests to minister. The next morning, as planned, two servants of God joined us for the prayer. They were ordinary men with minimum education. Pastor Yohannan (John), who is known for prophetic and healing ministry, and Pastor Kunjukunju, who was born blind and always needed assistance to move about or travel but was highly anointed by the Holy Spirit in the healing ministry. He was gifted at discerning and seeing visions of the heavenly and spiritual realms.

The prayer session for that day was concentrated on my deliverance and healing. A few more people outside of my family had also gathered in the room where we were in prayer. We started with some worship, followed by the sharing of the Word of God. After the Word was preached, the two visiting pastors started praying for me. The pastor who was blind prayed and received the discernment through a vision about my physical and spiritual condition and spoke about it so that the other pastor could call out and rebuke each spirit that caused the various sicknesses, infirmities, and symptoms in my body. Then they cast out those spirits one by one in the name of Jesus Christ.

All the symptoms that I had were linked to spiritual afflictions caused by the spirits that demonized me through my many years of rebellious living, through bad soul ties with my many associations with friends that indulged and practiced rebellious attitudes and activities. In those days, I used to participate in many pagan or occult practices with the unbelieving community out of ignorance. I grew up with these people in our community, but I never knew that these practices were strictly against biblical Christian principles and forbidden for believers.

"So then, about eating food sacrificed to idols: We know that 'An idol is nothing at all in the world' and that 'There is no God but one'" (1 Corinthians 8:4).

"The thief comes only to steal and kill and destroy" (John 10:10). I had become an eligible candidate for the devil to use me to partake in all kinds of bad attitudes, practices, and habits. They came to steal my youth and destroy me by afflicting me with sickness and disease and eventually wanted to kill me.

But thanks be to our Lord Jesus Christ, who came to my rescue. He showed mercy towards me, rescued me from the clutches of the evil ones, saved and delivered me. When these anointed servants of the Most High God started praying over me, these principalities and powers of darkness that had claim to my life and were controlling my habits and thought processes had to leave by the power of God's Spirit that worked through them.

"Greater is He that is in me than the one who is in the world." As I had accepted Jesus Christ as my Lord and Savior, and renounced all my wicked ways, these demonic forces now had no legal authority to remain and torment me physically and spiritually. The anointed servants of God had the authority of the Word of God, through the power of the Holy Spirit, to drive out the demons in the name of Jesus Christ, the one who defeated Satan and conquered death. During the deliverance prayers by the servants of God, each demon that manifested pronounced the name related to each of the afflictions they had placed in me, and they left my body after manifesting with loud wails or noises.

I could finally feel the relief and lightness in my body and mind. The pain, fatigue, and symptoms that I struggled with for several months had now left. It seemed like all the demons that were tormenting me those past months had finally left, and I was now experiencing freedom through deliverance—a freedom that I had never experienced all through my youth and recent life.

After the servants of God cast out the many demons from me, they also prayed that I would be filled with the Holy Spirit, and I received the baptism of the Holy Spirit. That was such an awesome, supernatural experience, when the power of God manifested in my body as I trembled and moved, lifted and dropped down by His strength. My body was moving from one corner of the room to another—something that was humanly impossible. My weak hands and legs suddenly got stronger. I shouted out prayers to God in other tongues, a language that I couldn't understand. I was filled up with the Holy Spirit and was speaking in other tongues. I had received my prayer language. But I also received the gifts of the Spirit. I received the gifts of healing and casting out of demons, although I didn't realize it at that time.

The demonic spirits tormenting me left as I was filled with the Holy Spirit. No more symptoms of physical weakness. But strength arose. I could walk, jump, sing, shout, and dance with the joy of the Lord. This continued through the night. Suddenly, my life seemed to have changed on that one night, a transformation from months of being bedridden, needing help to even get out of bed even earlier that day. Now I could do anything I wanted to on my own. The very next day, I started walking down our street without any assistance. Such a powerful supernatural miracle. I continued staying with my family for a few more days and then returned to Dharwad.

I had a new energy and joy; my heart was filled with gratitude to God who delivered me, and I wanted to testify to everyone what the Lord Jesus did in transforming my life. God had now given me the boldness to witness.

When I reached Dharwad I felt like a new person. My colleagues and my boss, who was a medical doctor, were confounded and couldn't understand how I could have been healed so quickly and how I didn't show any more symptoms. They reluctantly agreed to allow me to return to full-time work. However, the vision in my damaged right eye was still bad and hadn't healed. My boss compelled me to take the medications that I was given prior to my leaving for Kerala. I requested that I didn't want to continue medication, but they still compelled me to take it.

In a few weeks after resuming work, my eye seemed to have blood gushing into the eyeball. This caused me to stop working and take a rest. Then I was sent to Vellore Medical College, a highly renowned medical center in South India, to seek further investigation about my damaged eye. They ran many tests, including a spinal tap liver biopsy. However, they said there was no cure. The chief ophthalmologist said, "You are lucky you have one eye!" I returned to Dharwad in disappointment. I kept working but with one eye.

Later, within two months, I had a similar incident in the eyeball. This time they sent me to a medical research facility at a Bangalore cantonment hospital. The chief doctor there, Dr. Harris, was from London, UK. They had received all the medical documents from my Vellore hospital results. They did some tests and studied my situation, but they too couldn't figure out what the problem with my eye was. They sent my records to Bangalore Medical College. Their conclusion from these research tests was that I had some specific bacteria that was infecting my eye. The bacteria were named Tuberculae Bacilli, which is related to Leprae Bacillus. I had been working among leprosy patients for the last ten years, and this could have been contracted from those exposures. I was allergic to these bacteria, which causes bleeding in the eye. The diagnosis was "vitreous hemorrhage in the eye." The bacteria were a foreign body in the eye, which caused the bleeding.

It was a questionable diagnosis, but it was an inconclusive one. But there was no known treatment at that time. I went back to work in Dharwad. The condition of my eye remained bad, and I had to struggle to keep up with work with my one good eye.

In those days, I started attending Christian evangelical and crusade meetings in Dharwad. I participated in such meetings with local missions. This conflicted with the Swiss Emmaus organization, which didn't want any of their employees getting involved in preaching the gospel, proselytizing, or converting people from other faiths to Christianity. My boss came to hear about this and confronted me about it. He had loved me and cared for me, but he gave me an option, saying that if I continued to profess my beliefs and testify to anybody by talking about the gospel, that would cost me my job. That would mean that I would be asked to resign and leave. It was a tough decision for me to make.

I made a decision. I chose to serve the Lord. I couldn't abandon what God really wanted me to do. It was time to leave the organization, probably time to leave Dharwad, to any unknown destination, job, or business, trusting in God and trusting in His divine plans and purposes for me. He had given me a new life in Christ, and I wanted to cherish that and follow Him rather than follow my organization's demands that I renounce my mission.

During my stay at Dharwad, I used to attend prayer fellowship with a small congregation of born-again believers. These believers, however, did not believe and teach about the baptism of the Holy Spirit, His power, or the manifestations. When I returned to Dharwad after I had received my deliverance and healing, I was a spirit-filled believer who had experienced the power and authority of the Holy Spirit baptism. I was now much stronger and bolder in my faith in Christ. I was also hungry to know God and experience His goodness. I was known to the church congregants as an unfortunate brother afflicted with sickness and blindness. However, being a new Christian, I lacked Biblical knowledge, as I had just begun learning about the Bible in my new journey with Christ.

One day, in an evening prayer meeting, in an atmosphere of prayer and worship, a sister was praying for me very sympathetically. I had been quite wounded in my spirit. I prayed in my heart, asking the Lord for His mercy and to heal and restore my blind eye if it was His will for me to be healed. If not, He could tell me that I had to live with one eye and be half-blind for the rest of my life. I remembered the apostle Paul who had written about the "thorn in his flesh" and how he had to endure it after he had asked the Lord thrice to take the "thorn" away.

After that prayer meeting fellowship, as I was walking in the dark to my apartment, I suddenly saw a bright light, like lightning in the sky. It was the headlight of a truck coming from the opposite direction to my path. I instantly recognized that it was the first time in eight months I could see something with my damaged eye!

The next morning, I was walking in the street covering my good eye. I was able to see some shadows with my damaged eye. However, after a few days, the vision in my damaged eye started improving further. I was now able to walk with my good eye closed and with my now improved eye that was damaged. In about two weeks, I could also read the Bible with both eyes. God had restored my sight! I was now no longer a half-blind person.

It took me many more years to find out God's purpose for that blindness during that season. Now I realize God's purposes for His believers are always for the good, as it is written in Jeremiah 29:*11*, *"'For I know the plans I have for you,' declares the Lord, 'plans to prosper you and not to harm you, plans to give you hope and a future.'"*

When no one could heal me, Jesus Christ came to my rescue. This was a great testimony to demonstrate the goodness of God, to glorify His name. I share this wherever I go so that it might inspire someone who is in such a hopeless and helpless situation.

When I was in my depths of hopelessness, miserable in my struggles, anguish, and distress, only Jesus Christ could help me. No medical science, doctors, or human powers could help restore my vision.

3.
ARMUGHAM'S STORY– HEALING BY JESUS' TOUCH

I had narrated an overview of this story in my other book, *A Handful of Clay in the Potter's Hand*, but I want to continue to share it in the context of what happened to this family and their future generations after his deliverance. This man was touched and inspired when he first heard my testimony of God's divine healing and deliverance from various physical and spiritual afflictions.

I like to share these older stories because of the impact they have on people today. Recently, I had the privilege of witnessing to a young professional about the supernatural healing power of Jesus Christ. This young professional is named Vivek, and he is the grandson of Armugham. Yes, the same Armugham in this story. And hearing me share the story he heard from his own family had a huge impact on him.

The original event happened several decades ago on one of my last working days in India, before coming to America. At that time, I was a staff nurse working with very sick patients, including those with leprosy and other communicable diseases. It was a rural area in Kumbakonam in Tamil Nadu state, southern India.

One day during the morning clinical staff meeting, the chief medical officer mentioned a very sick patient in our ward named Armugham. He was a young man in his early thirties with a wife and two young children. Armugham was suffering from an acute inflammatory condition with very painful open sores all over his body. He could not even sit up in bed. The chief medical officer said he had been in the hospital for four months being kept alive with high doses of steroids, but he was not going to live more than a day or two longer. That day he was moved to a room closer to the morgue in the hospital and his wife was told to go make arrangements for the funeral. Their village was far from the hospital, so she had left to go make the necessary arrangements.

Even though I worked in that hospital, I had never met this patient. After the staff meeting, we all got busy with our work, but this man's condition was in my heart, so I waited until my shift was over and then went to his room, not really knowing what to expect.

As I entered his room slowly, he opened his eyes and glared at me. Even after ten years working in that environment, I had not seen a patient in such an acute condition. As I walked closer to his bedside and stood still for a few minutes, I could see tears coming from his eyes. I really didn't know how to console someone like him who was terminal and helpless. While I have been able to speak the consoling words of Jesus many times now, back then, I really didn't know how to console someone like him who was helpless and hopeless. From his name and appearance, I could tell that he was an upper-caste Hindu.

After a few moments of standing there, I broke the silence. "I know a physician who helped me when I was going through a difficult time, very sick with unknown sickness and a blinded eye. No one could help me, but I heard about Jesus Christ. When I called upon Him, He healed me from all that I was going through. He is my God who healed me with His supernatural power.

His eyes opened wide with hope, wanting to know more about this doctor who could heal. He was now anxiously eager to know how this doctor could heal him of his sickness. However, I also realized that it was getting late and dark outside and I still had to ride my bicycle for about five miles to my little rented hut to be with my wife Susie, who was pregnant and nearing her due date for delivery.

I continued to stand in the room thinking about what to tell him next, but I also realized that outside it was getting darker by the moment. I still had to ride my bicycle for about five miles to my little rented hut to be with my wife, Susie. She was pregnant and nearing her due date. I couldn't stay much longer. "I would like to pray with you before I leave," I said.

He agreed, and I prayed. Both of us were crying as I called out to the Jesus who had healed me and asked Him to do the same for this man. Before I said goodbye, I gave him the small New Testament Bible I kept in my pocket.

The next morning, I came back early, so I could visit with him. I was not sure what to expect, so I walked quietly to his room, but to my surprise, he was sitting in bed for the first time by himself.

As soon as he saw me, he said, "I didn't sleep at all last night. I have been reading the Bible you gave me. I want to know this Jesus more."

"Do you want to ask Jesus Christ to come into your heart and life?"

"Yes," he said.

With full submission he repeated the sinner's prayer and received Jesus as his personal Savior. When we finished praying, we both had tears in our eyes.

I was still a new Christian myself and didn't realize how perfectly this had happened, but I knew it was all God's will and his appointed time. That night after work, I was leaving for three days to have my visa interview and medical exam to get my immigrant visa to go to America.

I said goodbye to him without knowing whether I would ever see him again or not. That night I boarded the train for Madras (Chennai now), traveled through the night, completed my interview the next day, and received my immigration visa to come to America the same afternoon. Then I purchased a Tamil Bible and returned to Kumbakonam, where I lived with my wife Susie.

As soon as I returned, I went to see my wife and then rushed over to the hospital to see Arumugam. He was walking in his room and told me his doctor said that since he was doing so much better, maybe he could go home the next day. His sores were starting to heal and there was no more drainage. His swollen body had reduced in size. I was very happy and thanked God for healing him. He was looking very relieved as well and was happy and excited to go back to his family after spending four months in that hospital waiting for death.

The next morning was Saturday. I told him if he were released from the hospital, to come see me, so I could give him the Bible I had bought for him in his language. I marveled that in four days he had gone from preparing for death to starting a new life.

He had been both physically and spiritually dead, but now he was healed and alive in Christ. He inherited eternal life with the living God. With full hope and joy, he left for Pondicherry, which was a day's travel by bus. Just two days later, my very pregnant wife, Susie, and I left for Kerala, thus finishing my contract with Sacred Heart Hospital in Kumbakonam—the last place I was employed in India, before moving to America. Just a few weeks later, Susie gave birth to our beautiful daughter.

But our story did not finish there. Although I went to America and there was no Internet or telephone like today, I occasionally kept in contact with Arumugham through letters. He eventually was completely cured of his incurable disease and went back to work at his old job as a certified public accountant for a large company. His two children grew up, married, and they have their own families now. God restored all that he had lost to this disease because he came to know a living God. On our vacation trip from the United States to India, we stopped in Madras, where he came to meet us after twelve years. It was a miracle. He gave me pictures of his children and grandchildren playing in the park.

In fact, he continued to work for more than eighteen years with his company and lived twenty-five good years before he died. He saw many blessings from God during that season, and I wept in my office when I heard that he had passed away. I never considered him as a leprosy patient, but as a friend and brother in Christ. He gave me a chance to see and experience the marvelous handiwork of God. This was especially important early in my Christian life in ministry. God showed me that nothing is impossible with Him.

What is beyond miraculous is that this healing came to a man who had never even heard of Jesus Christ. He came to know Jesus and to live for Him as a result. During one of our mission trips to India, Arumugam's son, Murali, came to Kerala, where we were ministering and he too accepted Jesus Christ as his Lord and Savior. I had the privilege of baptizing him in the name of the Father, Jesus Christ the Son, and the Holy Spirit. That brings me to the beginning of this story and Vivek.

Many years later, in 2017, a young man from Houston called and introduced himself as Vivek, a computer engineer.

He said his mother had asked him to contact me. I invited him to our home. During our conversation, he said he wanted to know what I told his grandfather, Arumugam, whose life was changed by my prayer.

So I took Vivek to my office, and I shared our story. I also told him about what Jesus had done for his grandfather. After listening carefully, we both knelt, and he invited Jesus into his life as well. A few days later I took him to Lakewood Church in Houston, where I baptized him in water.

In 2019, during our mission trip to Orissa, we stopped in Chennai where Vivek invited his entire family, including Arumugham's wife, over and we had a fellowship meeting there.

In this book you will hear many such powerful stories of healing, deliverance, and lives changed by Jesus Christ. Each one of these stories has already changed hundreds of lives and villages, but they continue to change more lives each time they are told. There is power in the name of Jesus, and there is power in our testimony. I share these stories with you, having been a witness to them and the lives changed through the name of Jesus Christ and those who surrender to His Lordship.

"We will not hide them from their descendants; we will tell the next generation the praiseworthy deeds of the Lord, His power and the wonders He has done" (Psalm 78:4).

God healed Naaman, the commander of the Syrian army through prophet Elisha (2 Kings 5:1–14).

"And there were many in Israel with leprosy in the time of Elisha the prophet, yet not one of them was cleansed—only Naaman the Syrian" (Luke 4:27).

4.

A TWIN SISTER DYING
OF KIDNEY DISEASE

Around the year 1999, I was in my home in Houston, Texas during my morning prayer time when I remembered a phone call my wife had told me about. It had come from a neighbor I grew up with in India, but who was now living in New York. He had recently been diagnosed with prostate cancer, so I chided myself for forgetting to return his call when Susie first told me about it. When I called him, his wife answered. I had never met her, but as soon as I told her I was from Houston, she poured out her heart.

"My sister is dying. My twin sister is in Chennai, India, dying. She was in the hospital for about four and a half months, and the doctor told the family to take her home because they couldn't do anything more for her. They told her that both of her kidneys failed. She was undergoing dialysis daily, yet her condition was deteriorating."

It came out in a rush of emotion like a single sentence. She told me how several times her sister's shunt failed, and she had many complications while at the hospital. My friend's wife continued by saying that the doctor said it might be better to go home to die instead of dying in the hospital. The woman was a widow with two sons and a daughter living with her.

"I am planning to go to India next week on a mission trip," I told her, marveling at God's timing. "If you give me the address and the phone number, I'll go visit her while I am in India."

She gave me the phone number, and I promised I would go visit her sister when I was in Chennai, the big metro city in the large southeast Indian state of Tamil Nadu.

Normally, when I'm visiting a city, the friends I have in the area pick me up from the airport and take me to the hotel or to someone's home, where they arrange to hold prayer meetings for me to conduct before my next flight. I make the most of each trip, and though I may only stay in one place for a few days, I minister as much as I can there to make the trip fruitful and productive.

On this visit to Chennai, a Tamil speaking friend and construction contractor picked me up at the airport. He took me straight to the hotel so I could leave my luggage there and call the family before going to visit the sick woman.

It was a difficult journey to her home. There was a great deal of dirt and trash along the roads, and there was no way to reach her actual house by car, so we had to park the car and walk a great distance to get to the house where she lived.

Finally, we reached the home in Pallavaram where her adult children, two sons and a daughter, were waiting for me. The woman I had come to see was probably in her mid-fifties, lying on a hospital bed in the middle of the little family room. There was an IV bag running dialysis fluid into her. I was told she was on dialysis seven days a week because she was in kidney failure. One eye was completely shut and she could no longer open it. With the other eye, she looked at me in great distress.

As soon as I sat down, she began to share her difficult story with me. Her husband had passed away four years prior. Since then, the family had struggled to meet their needs. Her sons were working themselves to exhaustion, doing hard labor to make a living for the family. Her thirty-four-year-old daughter had once had a small job, but she quit her job to care for her mother. All her children were unmarried and single. They lived in a small, two-room home with little else. Their house was on the side of a street with adjacent houses. The road was very dusty and unclean. The homes were open and very close together, so much so, I could hear the conversations from other houses.

As I continued to listen to this dear lady, two older neighbors came over. Then a few more neighbors joined them. Soon, all the neighbors were crowding around the home and many of them came inside. Some thought she had passed away, while others wanted to watch and see what was going on.

This was a Christian family of believers. As the conversation progressed, I put my hands on my head and felt such pity for the entire family. They were going through so much. Her story continued from one tragedy to another. I was fully convinced the enemy had stolen all the goodness and joy from their lives.

Finally, I told her I didn't want to hear anymore. For the previous thirty-nine years, my ears had been filled with the sad stories of people. I was becoming angry in my spirit, not towards this poor lady or her family, but the power of darkness, the enemy, who had brought them to this level.

I was saddened in my spirit, and suddenly sadness gripped and overwhelmed me. I started crying out to God for mercy.

"Lord, the enemy has stolen everything from them. When are you going to restore their life?" I cried and pleaded with the Lord. I closed my eyes and turned my face to heaven and cried for this family. It went on like that for at least twenty to twenty-five minutes.

When I opened my eyes, I saw the room was filled with people. Everyone that came fell on the ground; some of them were crying along with me, some of them stood amazed. Others looked around, not comprehending what was going on. They couldn't understand why we were crying out since the woman was still alive.

I turned around and saw the sick woman sitting on the bed, dangling her feet down over the side. The room was filled with people lying down on the floor and weeping or praying, so at first, I didn't realize the significance of what was happening. Suddenly, she pulled out the tubes and ran to her kitchen.

"I haven't seen my kitchen for six months," she cried out. Then she came running back to the living room, much to our total astonishment. This woman, who had been bedridden less than an hour before, was now running back and forth because she was filled with joy as the Lord delivered her from death. Everyone who was lying on the floor crying wanted me to pray for them, and so I laid hands on everybody and prayed. I continued to minister and pray for the family and all the people in the house.

Things slowly calmed down and got quieter. We all had seen and experienced the awesome supernatural miracle that had just taken place. Eventually, it was evening and getting darker, so we began leaving for my hotel. The sick woman felt so much relief that she stood up to walk with us on our way out to the street!

The next morning, I left for my home state of Kerala and enjoyed two months of ministry in various places across the state. When I returned home from my trip, I received a detailed email from the sick woman's son. He wrote, "I would like to share with you what has happened to my mom. The week after your visit, we took her to the doctor. After doing a routine checkup, the doctor said that she is healed. She doesn't even need dialysis. The doctor was so shocked and surprised that he was not able to even say what precautionary medication should be prescribed. But he went on to do two days of dialysis instead of the routine seven days. Yet there was no sign of any kidney failure."

But the woman's miracle continued even after that first touch, because I revisited the family about a year later, and they were doing much better. Some relatives had come and furnished their home very nicely, and their finances had also begun to improve. It was so great to see the Lord blessing them. Later, I heard that the thirty-four-year-old daughter had married a very handsome man, and that marriage was far beyond their expectations.

After her daughter's marriage, the woman continued her checkups every six months, and her condition remained stable. I received regular emails from her son, which allowed me to help them financially, spiritually, and emotionally.

Several years later in 2005, I was planning to go to India with my wife. It was on this trip I finally learned the woman's name was Rosamma. In all the communication and miracles, I forgot to ask her name, but God knew it, and He loved her and delivered her.

Rosamma invited us to their house for dinner. It was then I finally learned her name. When we arrived for the meal, we saw Rosamma in great health. She was happy and hopeful. Despite what must have been a large expense, she cooked us rice and curry. The woman who five years ago couldn't leave her bed and was in a terrible financial crisis, had now cooked a meal for us with her own hands and served it to us. We sat down for dinner, and she joined us as well.

She was so eager to serve the servants of God. We were so honored that she had invited us for dinner. The meal was delicious. We stayed in that city, ministering in different places in the area. When it was time for us to leave, Rosamma sobbed with gratitude.

"Five years ago I was dying, and the doctor told me I would be dead within a few days. They sent me home to die with loved ones. Then you came and prayed for me. That incident changed my whole life. I was healed. My daughter is married, and she now has a child. I have seen my children being blessed, and I got to see my grandchild. My son is getting married this year. The other son got a higher promotion in his job in a computer company and his family is doing well."

Over the years, I believe she has had more grandchildren. When her younger son got married, they sent me a picture of everybody standing together—with Rosamma standing in the middle of the group. God had restored all the blessings she had once lost, and she was able to live and experience the goodness of God. She was able to rejoice in her blessings and thank God for all the things He had done in her life and the life of her family.

I heard she passed away on December 17, 2009. She was supposed to die ten years earlier, but the Lord God Almighty extended her life for a full decade. During that decade, she saw the destruction of the enemy's plan, and instead of the downfall of her family, she tasted the love, care, and blessings of God throughout her remaining earthly life. She saw the well-being and the prosperity of her family and her children restored. The Lord arranged everything so she could enter into her final rest in peace.

I am so thankful to God that He enabled me to be a battle-ax for Rosamma and her family.

Scripture References: Mark 5:22–43; Matthew 9:18–26; Luke 8:41–56.

5.
A WOMAN WITH KIDNEY TUMORS HEALED

It doesn't matter the person, place, or the illness because in every way the enemy's purpose is the same—destruction. Exposing the deception of the enemy and the illness and pain he puts on people is how you can remove it and gain victory. When I was called to go back to my people in 1993, one of my first mission trips was to Mumbai, the hugely populated big metro city in western India.

When I was called to minister, I had no formal training as a minister. I was a faithful member of my church, but that was all. Nobody knew me in India, and I had been away for over thirty years. The only people I knew were pastors who came to America and visited me or people I had helped previously.

One of these pastors I had met earlier was Pastor Thomas, who was based in Mumbai. In 1994, during my second mission trip to India, God showed me that He could work through me, no matter how weak I am. I had taken the long flight from Houston to Mumbai and arrived there around 2:00 a.m. local time. After two hours in immigration and customs, Pastor Thomas, who received me, drove me to his home for a short break and to drop off luggage. Brother Rajan, a relative of Susie, met me at Pastor Thomas's home and took me to the local train station, where we took a ten-hour train ride to Ankleshwar, a town in the western state of Gujarat. They had not booked a sleeper car on the express train, but it was a rather slow, local, basic passenger train that stopped at all stations. We sat on a bench and had to stand up at each of the stops to shift around. I was completely exhausted when we finally stopped at our destination, Ankleshwar. But after all the long flights and the train trip, it was now time to walk to our destination—brother Rajan's home!

I had traveled for more than two days without sleep. My mind was muddled from fatigue, but somehow, I kept moving forward. Finally, after a short walk, we came to a little one-room house where brother Rajan and his family lived. When I got there, they encouraged me to go rest, but the small house quickly filled with smoke from the wood fire stove in the kitchen. That, coupled with the high humidity and pollution, made it nearly impossible to sleep—even in my exhausted state. After taking some little refreshments, I fell asleep for a short nap. After an hour or so, they woke me up. I had to return to Mumbai later that night.

Brother Rajan's wife told me there was a tumor on her right kidney. The doctors had been observing it for three years, and it was continuing to grow and was very painful for her. The doctors told her she should have surgery, but she couldn't afford it, so she went every three months or so for an ultrasound scan. They were hoping I could pay for the operation, and indeed I had no problem helping, so I gave her the money she needed.

I also shared with them how God had healed my blinded eye in addition to several different sicknesses in my body and how He restored my life from all kinds of demonic afflictions and powers of darkness. And how God has now commissioned me to go about preaching the gospel and doing the supernatural things by His power and anointing. I shared my testimony and encouraged them that God has no limits, unlike humans. Brother Rajan and his wife were Christians but had never experienced any supernatural physical healings before. After I shared my testimony, I prayed. I said I believed—and believe—that God has no limits. Before I left, I placed my hand on her and prayed. I asked the Lord to heal her and then I left for Mumbai.

After that visit, I didn't see or hear from them for about two years, until the day when I saw Brother Rajan's wife at a hospital where she was caring for her mother-in-law. She recognized me instantly, and her eyes brightened.

"Brother," she said, "we wanted to write to you and tell you what happened after you came and prayed for me."

"Tell me," I said. "I am always happy and eager to hear a praise report." She was clearly doing well.

"It was a miracle," she began. "After you gave us the check, we took it to the bank. We had to wait for it to be processed before we could schedule the surgery. That took a little bit of time, but as soon as it cleared, I went to the hospital to schedule the appointment. They said they did not need to do any pre-op procedures because I had a confirmed diagnosis for months, so the doctors didn't redo any of the tests. On the day of my surgery, I was taken to the anesthesia room and then wheeled into the operating room. Of course, that is all I remember, but when I woke up I was told that before the surgeon did his first incision, he wanted to confirm he was in the right place, so they did an ultrasound to find where on my kidney the tumor was, but there was nothing. The kidney tumor was gone! I was sent home without having the operation and I've been fine these last two years."

"Completely healed?" I asked, not doubting God, but wanting to hear it again, as I was very excited. She said, "Completely! The tumor has totally disappeared, and I am fine. I have no symptoms or problems of any kind."

At that point, I had seen miracles before, but this was unique. Yet another story of a person God touched with supernatural healing and brought to a deeper faith in Christ.

On another trip to India in later years, I was visiting my wife's family in the same area in Ankleshwar and Brother Rajan came and shared how God completely healed his wife after I prayed for her.

I had just shared my testimony and said a short prayer. But God did the work. God can work beyond our human limitations or understanding to perform amazing miracles.

Scripture References: Mark 3:7–21; Matthew 12:15–16; Luke 6:17–19.

6.
AN INOPERABLE THYROID TUMOR HEALED

Cherikkal was our "Samaria," as that was the place where the lower-caste people lived. Caste is a major consideration, even in modern-day Indian Hindu society. As has been the case for centuries, the lower caste usually won't mingle and live among the upper castes, apart from providing skilled or unskilled labor. Casteism has not been fully eradicated in modern times and can transcend from Hindu to Christian communities, too. It impacts relationships, marriages, religion, and businesses.

There was no relationship between the lower and upper castes in my state of Kerala in those days, including among the Christian community. It was our mission to evangelize this group of people, being we were traditional denominational Christians. Nobody dared to go into their community.

This is the life story of Omana, who is a believer in our church at Pandalam, Kerala. She was one of the first few believers I prayed with who came to the knowledge of Christ through a miraculous healing. At that time, she was a young woman who was married, with one child. Though her healing miracle happened more than fifteen long years ago, the memories of it remain vivid for me today. When the miracle occurred, she was in her mid-thirties and working for the school. She belonged to a Dalit or Harijan lower caste Hindu family, who were called "untouchable" in the past.

Omana came to the saving knowledge of Christ through her physical problem. She had a large tumor on the right side of her neck, but I was told she could not undergo surgery for it because the doctors determined it was too risky to operate. The orange-sized tumor was a burden for her, and she could not even walk because of it.

I am sure she had prayed many prayers and gave sacrificial offerings to her Hindu gods without any relief. Desperate for help, she even went to several medical colleges hoping they'd be willing to do the surgery, but even the doctors there said it was very risky to operate. She suffered not only physical pain but also social stigma because of the large tumor's effect on her physical appearance.

One day, we met her in the home of a Christian believer who was a part of our ministry. By that time, she'd decided there was no other hope for her. Her many prayers and offerings had done nothing. Omana had heard that we could pray for her, and she was ready to believe what we were saying. She came with great anticipation of being healed. When we presented Jesus Christ, the Healer, she gladly received and believed in Him. When she came to Christ, she also believed that she would be healed.

The day we prayed for her, she said that she felt something in her body, as if the tumor was dissolving. She said the tumor was shrinking, but we could not see any difference. However, a few days later it had completely withered away. She had a miraculous healing in her body, and she became totally healthy.

After this she became very enthusiastic in her witnessing for Christ. When people have an encounter with Christ, it is easy to get excited and enthusiastic. She also had a great burden for her household, so she invited us to her house. Her father and her other relatives all lived around her small little hut. We shared the gospel with them, and they came to the saving knowledge of Christ as well.

Thereafter, she became a living witness in her neighborhood and to the entire village of Cherikkal. Hundreds of people came to Christ, and we were able to start a church. Although it was a small, rural community, once we started the church—just in front of Omana's house—the persecutions started. The local community was almost entirely Hindu.

Believers were harassed when they tried to go to the church, but many people still participated with great enthusiasm and a hunger to receive God's Word. They were not disappointed because those who braved the persecution received miraculous healing and deliverance.

We were not simply ministering to them spiritually. We were trying to meet the physical needs of the community as well. We did charitable work there by building several houses for the poor people and repairing many other houses. We supplied clothing, food, and even supported the needy financially. Though many had previously attempted to work among this community, the Lord enabled us to establish the first church in Cherikkal.

Often, when people in poor, rural areas come to faith, they need financial support. Usually, these people are isolated from the community, and they need all kinds of support, as well as protection. We did all these things wholeheartedly. As a result, a good number of people from these areas were saved and came to the church. We had new believers from all walks of life receiving Christ through our ministry: Orthodox, Brahmin (or upper castes), and Dalit (lower castes).

As the church developed into a community that included

people from a variety of backgrounds, we faced some cultural and community problems within the church. Historically, apart from the caste system based on Hinduism, a person's skin color and education level also determined who they were permitted to associate with, what their job type would be, and many other related things. There was no way to move up in the social classes. In fact, just like in the Bible, a person with leprosy had to cry out when they carried the disease. But through Christ, they were no longer bound to these limitations. The old ways had been practiced for centuries, however, so it required members to renew their minds with God's Word and grow into this truth.

In fact, not all the believers were happy to have fellowship with the Dalit lower caste community, though most of the upper caste origin believers welcomed it. The opponents were sticking to their old social status and lifestyle, despite coming to faith in Christ.

We continued to minister, however, because it is only the true work of salvation, not just theology and doctrines, that can change a culture and people. We knew we could not change a community's morals in a single day. It would be a long process and for that, they needed time and support. However, when we started this church, despite the opposition of some, we lived and practiced what Jesus taught.

Omana came from Hinduism, but she was now firm in her faith in Jesus Christ and, because of her faithfulness, God saved everyone in her family. Initially, her husband strongly opposed the church, but eventually, he accepted Christ, and the Lord enabled me to baptize him, her son, daughter, and father. They were all baptized together and together they joined the fellowship with us.

Soon after the baptism, Omana and her family faced many problems, including the death of her husband. Yet, Omana stood strong, and she never wavered in her faith. In fact, I would call her up to the front of the church when I prayed for people with tumors, because she had experienced healing from that condition, and when she shared her testimony of healing with them, it lifted the faith among the congregants. She also understood the pain and shame they were experiencing. God blessed her family, too. Her daughter's wedding ceremony and celebration was one of the best that was ever solemnized in that area. Once you start to serve the Lord, God will exalt you. Omana and her family were not rich or wealthy people, but oh, how God has changed their lives.

"In all this you greatly rejoice, though now for a little while you may have had to suffer grief in all kinds of trials. These have come so that the proven genuineness of your faith—of greater worth than gold, which perishes even though refined by fire—may result in praise, glory and honor when Jesus Christ is revealed" (1 Peter 1:6–7).

Scripture References: Mark 3:7–21; Matthew 12:15–16; Luke 6:17–19.

7.
AN AIDS PATIENT HEALED

Our God is a wonder-working God. We saw another example of this in Jalna, a district in the eastern region of the state of Maharashtra in western India. Pastor Samuel, a senior evangelist in the region, and I were traveling through the villages of Jalna when we reached one of the suburbs not far from the big town. This was our final Sunday meeting of that trip. The only place we could find to have the meeting was on the rooftop of an unfinished three-story building. A few Bible school students from Kerala, a school manager, and a lot of local village folks were in attendance.

Pastor Samuel was doing foundational work in that area so he could establish a congregation. Most of the believers were villagers and some of them were from the slum area of Jalan town, too. They all came to the meeting full of enthusiasm and anticipation of what God would do. The weather was nice enough to allow us to conduct the meeting on the roof and enjoy the breeze.

Even before the meeting started, many people came forward for prayer. We told them we would have time for prayer after the service. We did that because many of the people were new believers. They would come to the meetings at the beginning to get prayer and then leave without hearing the teaching. It is very important for them to be fed by Biblical teachings and not just come to get physical needs met.

As the Sunday service progressed, a man in his early fifties was brought in on a cot. Four people carried him, and they were followed by the man's parents, children, wife, and family members. They had carried him on a cot, climbing up three floors of stairs, to the roof of the three-story building where we were meeting. The man was too weak to even sit up. The pastor knew him well, and he told me that he was dying of AIDS.

This was a traditional Marathi family. They were all very concerned about his health. The relatives did not have any prejudice about AIDS. His mother, a traditional Maratha woman dressed in traditional clothing, came and spoke to me. Her son had not eaten food for four months and barely drank anything during that time. She wanted me to pray for him. He was clearly in the last stage of his life. I agreed to pray.

The rooftop didn't have much space, but I asked the crowd to make enough room for the cot to be laid down. I was the main guest and one among a few pastors who would share the Word that day. Therefore, everyone moved around until the new group was accommodated and then we continued the service.

At the end of the meeting, people lined up for prayer. I went and prayed for the AIDS patient by laying my hands on him and praying the Word over him. After that, I prayed for his family, too. Then, I turned to the others who were waiting for prayer.

Many healings and miracles happened in that place that day. A deaf girl was healed. As soon as I touched her, her ear popped, and she said she could hear. There was a patient with advanced cardiac problems so severe that he could barely make it up to the roof of the building, but after prayer, he said he was much better. The line of people waiting for prayer was extensive, and it took us hours to pray for all of them. This is usually the case in many similar meetings across the countryside.

After the service, we served food to everyone because the villagers had traveled quite a distance and there weren't any restaurants or places to eat. The brothers served the people by cooking for the group and serving the meal on the ground floor of the building. While I was coming down from the roof, I saw the man with AIDS sitting on the second floor, together with his family members. People were sitting around him and eating goat mutton biryani—an Indian delicacy typically reserved for special occasions. This man who had not been able to eat for four months had a big handful of food and he was going to put it in his mouth. I was astounded!

Seeing me, his mother motioned me with her hand and said, "Look, look, my son is eating food now. He is able to eat food!"

I said, "God has touched him, healed him and now he can eat anything he wants, and he can do whatever he wants to." I thanked God for his life.

I also went and got some food, and as I was eating, I watched the man, once too weak to walk, now walking out to a car. He turned and came back to me. We talked together for a bit with the help of an interpreter. I told him that Jesus had healed him.

"Be faithful to God, go and share this with your family and bring them to salvation. Save your whole family." He left for his village, and we went back.

Later, I heard that his family came back to talk to the pastor, and they took him to their village. They wanted to know more about Jesus Christ, the One who healed an AIDS patient. The pastor used this opportunity to talk about Jesus, and their entire family got saved, water baptized. Eventually, they started a fellowship in their home. Furthermore, because of this miracle, the first church was established in that village.

God has different ways of establishing His church and he has a different means of doing things for people. A traditional Maharashtrian family who had never heard or experienced the love or healing power of Christ was delivered instantaneously. That man was the head of the family and because of it, God used him to establish a church in that village. Since that time, I haven't had much opportunity to go to Jalna, but Pastor Samuel is doing great ministry in that region. Many churches have been established over the years in that area under his leadership.

"There he found a man named Aeneas, who was paralyzed and had been bedridden. 'Aeneas,' Peter said to him, 'Jesus Christ heals you. Get up and roll up your mat.' Immediately Aeneas got up. All those who lived in Lydda and Sharon saw him and turned to the Lord" (Acts 9:33–35).

What a mighty God we serve! He is a God of compassion and love. Let all glory be unto Him forever and ever.

8.
A HEALING STORY IN RAHURI

A young doctor shared his testimony during a baptism service in the Rahuri town, Ahmednagar district of central Maharashtra. We had meetings arranged in a large community center, and many came for worship and to hear the gospel. There were also people who had been saved in the meeting, so we were preparing for a large group for water baptism.

One of those being baptized that day was a young medical doctor from that village who was born into a Hindu family. While he was from that village, he was also affiliated with medical centers in Pune, a large industrial city in that region. When he came forward, we asked him to share his testimony before his baptism.

He shared the story behind his salvation and his decision to be water baptized:

"My mother had been diagnosed with terminal cancer. Initially, being a physician, I tried to treat her, but eventually I took her to Pune Medical Center College Hospital for treatment by a specialist. She was treated for some time there but was eventually told that there wasn't much more they could do for her. The treatment was not going to cure her cancer. We brought her back to the village and continued treatment at home.

"One day, one of our ministry leaders, Pastor Balu Borde, was visiting homes and praying for people. Somehow, he ended up at the home where my mother was staying. The pastor asked if he could pray for her. She agreed and that day my mother felt better. The pastor continued to visit regularly and each time he would pray, she would begin to feel a bit better. Gradually over a period of days, her condition improved. I asked my mother how it happened, and she told me about the pastor and the prayers."

(Pastor Balu Borde's deliverance and supernatural transformation is mentioned in a separate story in this book titled *A Criminal Becomes an Evangelist*.)

This testimony is an example of one of the many ways we reach people who are practicing other religions. We pray for the sick and share the love of Christ, who heals.

During the altar call, this young doctor continued his story:

"I am a physician who treated my mother. I took her to a medical college specializing in cancer research and they treated her, but nothing they did worked, and we had no hope for healing. That is when this pastor started praying for my mother and she was healed by Jesus Christ.

"We also have gods of our own, and we prayed and made all kinds of sacrifices and performed religious rituals for my mother's healing, but nothing happened. Here, an unknown person coming and talking about an unknown God produced results. When everything else fails, there is a God who can change things, who can heal the sick, and even people who are dying. Our gods did not help my mother, so if this God can help, why should I believe in any others? So I made the decision to serve Him. That is why I have decided to accept Him as my personal Savior. Now, according to the Word, I made the decision to take water baptism, and I want to be a Christian. A Christian means serving the Lord Jesus Christ."

I was amazed by this testimony. I did not know what to say

of such a practical faith. God is working with these people and manifesting His power among the Gentiles for their salvation.

On that day, we baptized about sixteen people, and we have now established several very active churches in that region.

One miracle of God can save a village, or many villages, or even a town. A living testimony has a lot of power. God healed that woman, and He changed her entire situation; she is a living testimony in that village. Because of God's timely manifestation of His power, that village and district came to the knowledge of Christ.

9.
HEALING OF SICKLE CELL ANEMIA

Sickle cell anemia predominantly affects a particular group of people in certain African tribes, particularly younger people. It is a hereditary disease of the red blood cells. It causes a shortage of the blood supply to vital organs and bone cells and causes vital organs to shut down. During a crisis, there are severe episodes of crippling pain in the hands and feet. This disease leads to a very short life expectancy, often resulting in premature death.

According to the *American Medical Journal*, the sickness is also observed in the Northeastern region of India among the Kui tribe in the eastern Indian state of Odisha. I have heard that nearly 30 percent of the local population of that tribe could have been affected by this disease.

In 2008, during the great persecution of Christians in Kandhamal, Odisha, our ministry sent a group of pastors to the affected people to provide aid to this persecuted group of Christian refugees. Most of these Christians belong to the Kui tribe. To this day, we are continuing our work with these indigenous tribal Christians by supporting the pastors and their families and providing educational support to children. The purpose of our visit was to follow up on the progress of the work there, to encourage and invigorate our newly established churches. Most of the damaged church buildings were burned. Initially, we helped rebuild eight church buildings that were destroyed by the anti-Christian rebels.

During a 2013 visit to Kandhamal, Odisha, while we were praying for people in a village meeting, a young girl about thirteen years old who had been diagnosed with sickle cell anemia inflammatory condition came with acute pain in her joints and a continuous fever. We prayed for her and then left the area a couple of days later after other meeting engagements. A few weeks later, the lead pastor wrote me a letter thanking me for praying for his daughter and telling me that the symptoms had disappeared, and she was feeling much better, so she stopped taking the medicine for her condition. However, the authorities from the school that she attended insisted on showing evidence that she was indeed fully healed from this incurable disease. So they asked her parents to take her for additional checks at the hospital that treated her, followed by the hospital in the big city, and finally at the medical college research facility. All tests and results came back negative.. Sickle cell anemia is an incurable sickness, and the person infected has a short life expectancy with a great deal of suffering from symptoms. In fact, many drop out of school because of related physical issues. But for this healed young girl, she finished high school and attended college. We witnessed a supernatural healing of an incurable disease. There is nothing impossible with a living God who can heal and restore life.

During our 2017 visit, Susie and I visited Kandhamal to minister in the local churches, orphanages, and participate in elementary school programs. We have a great number of pastors working in that area. We built or rebuilt ten churches in this part of Kandhamal. These persecuted and suffering faithful Christians are very active in evangelism and passionately worship with tears and hearts pouring out.

During our visit, the older daughter of Pastor Digal came forward and asked for permission to testify about her sickle cell disease ordeal. She was in her mid-twenties, a beautiful young lady who had suffered lots of pain from sickle cell disease. She experienced joint pain, fever, inflammation, difficulty breathing, and heart problems. She had to take a handful of pills every day very frequently.

This disease process is monitored by regular weekly blood tests. Since the prayer on our second visit in 2013, her symptoms had completely disappeared, and she was feeling perfectly well, as I mentioned above. On our third visit, we found out that she was completing her bachelor of science in nursing. Since then, she has completed education courses in 2022 and now she is a very healthy, very vibrant BSc nurse in her region.

In all my healthcare work—nearly fifty years—I have taken care of young people in crisis situations. Never have I heard such a beautiful work of God—all glory to Him, who can do things beyond our imagination.

What is beyond? A hereditary disease, incurable with medicine, healed by the power of God. The traditional and generational tribal curse was erased by the power of God, not only in India, but in the USA, Africa, and other parts of the world. Only Jesus' blood can wash away sin and sickness and break generational curses. Here is a living testimony for both believers and unbelievers, including medical professionals.

In Mark 5:25–34, we read about the awesome miracle of the woman who had been subject to bleeding for twelve years. She had suffered a great deal under the care of many doctors and had spent all she had, yet instead of getting better she grew worse.

But in the presence of Jesus, when she touched his garments, she immediately got healed and her chronic bleeding issue suddenly stopped. One touch from Jesus Christ is enough to heal, deliver, and set us free from years of afflictions. When we reach out to Him in faith, He won't let us down. He won't deny us the miracle.

10.
HEALING OF SEVERE ASTHMA

This happened in the fall of 2014.

Susie and I were visiting the capital of Macedonia, walking around in the marketplace. Susie found a children's shoe store and walked in. The shopkeeper was an elderly man who was standing and waiting on us. I noticed that he was having severe breathing difficulties, and he was gasping for air. So I walked closer to him and put my left hand on his shoulder and my right hand on his chest and started praying without making any commotion that would distract other customers. The man stood quietly for a few seconds and soon started breathing almost normally.

He asked me, "Do you think I can breathe normally through my nose?" Before this moment, he was able to only breathe with difficulty through his mouth.

I said, "Yes, you can certainly breathe through your nose."

Suddenly, the man started to breathe comfortably through his nose. He was healed and delivered from his physical affliction. I told him that I had prayed in the name of Jesus Christ and that He was the One who healed him.

He told me that he was a Muslim from Albania, which is in eastern Europe. I told him that Jesus loves Muslims and can heal them, too. He bore the sins and afflictions of all mankind, including Muslims, when He was brutally crucified.

The man listened and came and hugged me and said, "You are a good man." That is a high praise in the Muslim world.

But no one can be good, only Jesus Christ is and will ever be the One who is good. But He chooses to demonstrate His goodness through His disciples, when we are available and ready to do His calling, to pray for and serve others who are afflicted and oppressed.

We saw a Muslim man healed by the power and name of Jesus Christ. He had a great smile of gratitude when we left the store.

God had set this up for us. An appointment to bring him to an encounter with the true and living God, who healed and delivered him from his affliction.

HEALINGS AND BAPTISMS

"Whoever believes and is baptized will be saved, but whoever does not believe will be condemned. And these signs will accompany those who believe: In my name they will drive out demons; they will speak in new tongues, they will pick up snakes with their hands; and when they drink deadly poison, it will not hurt them at all; they will place their hands on sick people, and they will get well" (Mark 16:16-18).

Early in our ministry, I was convinced that whoever received salvation should be baptized immediately, so we always encouraged people to be water baptized after receiving salvation. Over the years of my ministry, I have baptized thousands of people. During the baptisms, I have come across many different experiences. During these baptisms, there were signs, wonders, healing of physical and mental afflictions, and manifestations of demonic spirits that were controlling their behavior. We have often seen that before a person accepts Jesus Christ as their Lord and Savior, they may have been in bondage to demonic spirits that controlled and afflicted them physically and mentally, keeping them in long-term chronic sickness and with physical disabilities. When they obey God and publicly confess Jesus Christ as Lord and Savior and partake of water baptism, these demon spirits now no longer have claim over them. I am sharing with you a few of the noteworthy miracles that took place during water baptisms.

Serving in India can present unique challenges. Accepting one more deity or having a ritualistic immersion in water is not a problem to the Indian mindset. They will readily accept the idea of adding another god to the list of other gods they worship. However, our task is like what Paul encountered when he was evangelizing the Greek and Roman world. We must show that Jesus is not just another god, He is THE God of the universe, Savior of all mankind. He is the only One who died and bore the penalty for all human sin. When baptizing in the name of the Father, Son, and Holy Spirit, a divine intervention happens in that person's life. Paul said in Acts 17:23 that the people had an altar to an "unknown god," but he then pointed them to the true God. He told the people that they had to abandon the false gods they worshiped and serve the one true God and Him alone. We continue that work today through signs and miracles.

11.
HEALING OF CONGENITAL HEART DISEASE

In New Delhi there were several members of our church who requested that I baptize them. The group included both Indians and Nepalis (those who originated from the neighboring country of Nepal). On one such occasion, Tamang and his mother, two locals, came together to be baptized. After the baptism while I was praying for everybody, Tamang told me that he had a heart problem since childhood and experienced chest pain all the time, so I also prayed for his healing and we then left from there after the program.

That day, we had a national pastor's conference in New Delhi. There were many pastors who came from different parts of the country, but it was strictly for pastors and their spouses. Before starting the meeting, Tamang came to the conference and said he wanted to speak with me. He told me the heart problems I had prayed against that morning that had caused him constant chest pain since childhood seemed to have gone after our prayer for healing. He was also able to do many things that he couldn't do before.

"I am completely healed," he said.

What a wonderful testimony to receive just before speaking to a group of pastors, so we had him testify during the pastor's meeting. He told them about the congenital heart disease, its symptoms, and what had happened during prayer that morning. The pastors rejoiced and their faith was stirred up when they heard and saw this young man. I have continued to receive updates, and this young man completed high school and technical college and then went on to work in management. God has blessed him in many other ways. Now he is very active, working full time with youth and the music ministry in our church, where he continues to have a good future by God's grace.

12.
EPILEPSY HEALED AFTER BAPTISM

The following morning, we were supposed to have a meeting inside the house where we were staying. It wasn't a public meeting; it was just a small gathering at the house. A couple we had visited the previous day brought one of their sons, Pramod. He was about twenty-five years old and suffered from a seizure disorder of some kind his entire life. Every time he tried to go somewhere, he would start to have seizures. His illness limited what he could do and affected how others saw him.

The family dressed him to come meet us, but he could barely walk by himself because he always needed assistance. He was wrapped up in a couple of blankets and had a purple-colored shawl wrapped around him, giving him a "priestly" look. The pastor told me that Pramod's parents were new believers in Jesus Christ and they had brought their son there because they truly believed that Jesus could heal Him.

I walked over to shake his hand and observed that he was burning with fever. I worked in healthcare, so I knew he was very sick the moment I touched him. My medical understanding was that he should have been taken to see a doctor and get medical help at a hospital, but because of his parents' persistence and faith, we continued to proceed with his baptism.

"I cannot put someone this sick in the cold water," I said. My medical training told me that would be a very bad idea, but the faith of this young man and his parents was more persistent than my doubt.

"If anything happens," the father said, "we take full responsibility and will never blame you, but he will be baptized today."

Reluctantly, I agreed to baptize him in a little pond near the church with some other candidates. When it was his time to get in the water, it was very difficult. I baptized him in the name of the Father, Son, and Holy Spirit. When he came up, to our surprise, something had happened to him because he looked very different. His body temperature was down, and he looked so bright. All of us were surprised that this boy was completely healed when he took water baptism.

Later that evening, I reflected on the day. Those parents had more faith than I had for his healing. In fact, I had discouraged them from doing it, but God honored his parents' faith and healed him completely. Since then, Pramod assists the pastors in sharing the gospel every single day in the villages as one of the ministry assistants. Furthermore, despite a lifetime of seizures, he has not had a single epileptic attack since the day of his baptism.

I don't know how to explain what happened, but I have seen it with my own eyes. He remains a living testimony. Every time we meet, he is very active, something he had never been able to be before. So the blood and stripes of Jesus Christ healed a lifelong epileptic patient and turned him into an Evangelist. As a mission worker, he is a living testimony in the villages of Jalna, Maharashtra, India.

Scripture References: Mark 9:14–28, 30, 32; Matthew 17:14–19, 22, 23; Luke 9:37–45.

13.
SIMON THE MENTAL PATIENT GETS HEALED

In my early days ministering in Pandalam, Kerala, I was baptizing new believers in a small tank of water my father had built at his home. There were many people who came to be baptized on one particular day. At the end of the baptism, the pastors who worked with me brought a man for prayer who was a homeless mental patient known for wandering on the streets.

In those days, and perhaps even in many places today in India, people who had mental disorders were looked down upon in society, especially in rural areas and small towns. They were ostracized from society and people stayed away from them. They were sent to public facilities that provided limited care. Even their family members disowned them, as they thought this would be their state until the end of their life, and there was no hope for them. They were not treated with any respect and were isolated from normal human society.

Coming back to the case of the homeless and mentally ill person, on that day during the baptism program, one of the pastors had prayed for his deliverance. They told him that if he accepted Christ and received water baptism, he would be healed. They brought him to the water tank where I was still standing after baptizing many people. Personally, I didn't have too much faith to do that because I didn't know this man.

However, if my coworkers believed that this was going to happen, I agreed that God would honor their faith, and so he came down into the water.

He was a fragile, dark-colored man in his late thirties. He appeared to be coming from a lower caste Hindu background. I was concerned about his soul, so I closed my eyes as he stood in front of me, raised my hands, and prayed for him. While my hands were raised and I was still praying, this mentally unstable person submerged himself in the water, and he stood up, drenched from head to toe. He looked around, still in the water, laughing. Everyone was stunned at seeing this. This wasn't the laugh of the joy of salvation, but the laugh of a man who wasn't sane.

The people who brought him were in a daze because they never expected that to happen. I was also upset. Baptism isn't a joke and the spirits affecting this man were mocking us. Then, I took authority in Jesus' name and said, "I didn't baptize this man, he did it himself, but now I am going to baptize him in the name of the Father, the Son, and the Holy Spirit."

Then I baptized him. When I raised him up from the water, he came out a totally normal person. Under the authority and power of God, he was totally healed and delivered. It isn't the water or even going under the water; it is the authority of the name of Jesus. This spirit inside him tried to mock that, but Jesus had the final say!

Usually, I don't see the same people after I meet them because I keep on moving and going to different places and different events during my short trips to India. However, six months later, I went back on another trip. We planned to distribute some Bibles to our new believers and had more than 150 Bibles to distribute that day. People were standing all around the church to receive a Bible, so I asked them to make a queue and come one by one to receive their Bible.

I saw the same man standing humbly, moving forward in the queue to receive a Bible. When he came closer to me, my heart was broken. I was moved with God's compassion, and I couldn't hold my emotions. Displays of affection are unusual within the Indian culture, but I embraced him and started weeping. In tears I said, "Only the love of Christ has brought you here. Only the love of God could change you. I have the spirit of the Lord in me; that is why I can love you like this."

I am only Ipe, but I serve a mighty Jesus.

I freely admit that the day this man came to be baptized, I didn't really believe it would change him, but God is not limited by what I think or see. Man sees only the outward, but God sees the inside of a man. In my own power, I cannot convince anyone who Christ is. I leave that to the Holy Spirit and the power of the testimony that God has given me. I don't mind sharing how my life was, but there are times when I am reminded of my own weaknesses.

As the apostle Paul once said, "I come to you with great fear." For me, it is not a fear of man, but the fear of my inadequacy, of leaders, of not knowing the culture, and of not having a strong vocabulary. I came into the ministry with great fear and without a great knowledge of how to preach, but with humbleness, the only thing I preach and know to preach is Jesus Christ.

That is what I have done in many places. I preached what Jesus did in my life or in the life of other people. This unchanging God never left anyone who called upon His name. When I shared my testimony, some saw me as immature in the ministry, so they asked me with what authority I was doing all these things.

Once, an elderly believer came to me and asked me who had given me the authority to baptize people and who had laid hands on me to anoint me to do the ministry. I could have easily answered, but I didn't want to create a disagreement. All I said was, "Look around and you will see in whose authority I am doing all these things."

Many of them thought I was going to take believers from other churches to start a new church. We have a church planting ministry all over India, and we did not have to get any believers from any other churches to begin. All we had to do was go to the people and places where Jesus was needed. We weren't ashamed to go out and witness, and as a result, people from all over came to the knowledge of Christ. Whatever we said and shared with them, they found it to be true.

It has been nearly thirty years now that I've been ministering. I have come across many people, preached on many stages, and visited many villages and towns. My message has been clear, "Just try my God." So far, no one has questioned me, and I can say with all certainty, my God will never fail anyone who trusts in Him.

14.
POSTPARTUM PSYCHOSIS HEALED

This story took place during one of my visits in the late nineties. By that time, we had planted many outreach churches from the main church in Pandalam. Our pastors and evangelists would arrange many local meetings where I would share the gospel and pray for the sick and bound.

One day, a father and mother brought their married daughter for prayer in one of our outreach churches in Omalloor, near Pandalam. She was married, in her mid or late twenties, and was so mentally disturbed that she was sometimes violent. She was married to a man who worked in the Middle-East, and she had come back to India to have her first child with them according to the local customs. At full term, they took her to the local hospital and waited anxiously to have the baby. This was the young couple's first child, as well as the first grandchild for her parents. Sadly, the child was stillborn.

It upset everyone in the family, and they did not have the courage to tell her the news. The parents decided to bury the newborn without showing their daughter. When she was awakened, she asked for the baby, but her parents explained what they had done. She was completely inconsolable from pain and grief and even became very violent.

Meanwhile, her husband flew back from the Middle East to India to be with her and tried to comfort her when she came home from the hospital. She did not improve, however, and in fact, her condition was so bad that when it was time for her husband to return to the Middle East to work, her parents decided to keep her at their home.

Many prayers and offerings were made on her behalf at her parents' church, but without any result. About that time, one of our native workers learned their story and told them about the prayer meeting going on. It was difficult, but they brought her to our meeting. During the meeting, she became calmer and even participated in worship and accepted Christ at the end of the meeting. We had a good worship service before this and of the twenty-two people who made the long journey in a crammed van, nine were to be baptized that day. Among them was the young woman suffering from postpartum psychosis.

After the baptism, her parents invited us to their home for a cup of tea. We sat in the living room of their home and the parents were in tears, sharing with us the struggles of the previous year.

"We never knew what to expect from her. Many times, she would chase us with a kitchen knife to try to kill us," they said.

While they shared their story, their daughter went to the kitchen to prepare tea for all of us. "This is the first time ever since her delivery incident that she is going into the kitchen to do anything," her father said.

Is there anything too hard for the Lord? This young lady was completely healed and delivered from postpartum psychosis once she accepted Christ and was water baptized. It brought joy to that home and to her elderly parents. It was something to witness.

When God does something, God does it perfectly. We have seen the joy of that family, the restoration and satisfaction of that lady.

She said, "My God, my Jesus, took away that burden and

healed my heart and mind today. Now, I can go back to my husband and live with him."

After she made the decision to receive Christ, her parents got their normal daughter back, and the husband got his wife back.

Scripture References: Matthew 3:8 16–17; Luke 3:21–22; John 1:32–39.

15.
THE SPIRIT OF FEAR CAST OUT

On one Sunday church service in the Pandalam church, a man brought his daughter to the church service. She was in her mid-twenties and unmarried. Her mother had died a few years ago, and the father took care of all three kids and the household affairs. Since the mother's death, his daughter had struggled with constant fear. Now, as a woman, she continued to be afraid of everything. She turned her face down whenever someone looked at her and she was afraid of talking to people. When the family came to church, they all sat on one side and this girl never raised her head. Furthermore, she was so depressed, nobody could talk to her. During the worship portion of the service, we started to pray for her deliverance from fear. When we did, she crawled down like a snail and wouldn't talk or move. Finally, after a long time of prayer, she sat up. We could see she was possessed by some kind of evil spirit.

At the end of the meeting, we asked her if she wanted to accept Jesus Christ as her Lord and Savior. She agreed and recited the sinner's prayer. Then we talked about the need to be baptized. We wanted her baptized as a sign of salvation, but also because when there are demonic spirits or spirits of depression on a person, we've seen deliverance come through baptism. It took a great deal of persuasion because she was afraid to get into the water, but finally she was convinced and she and her father both agreed to be baptized. However, when it came time for her to enter the pool, she was terrified and refused to get in. The water was only about three feet deep, but despite everyone assuring her she was completely safe, she wouldn't get in. We continued with the other baptisms, while the ladies continued to try to reassure her.

Everyone else was baptized, but this young lady struggled with fear and resisted. But eventually she agreed to enter the water, and I held her hand as she did.

"I baptize you in the name of the Father, the Son, and the Holy Spirit," I said, but as I held her, she just drifted out of my hands and moved backwards in the tank and tried to climb out. She was scared.

This spirit of fear had a strong grip on her, but the name of Jesus had more power. For her, it would be about that small step of trust.

"I take full responsibility for your safety," I said. "I promise that you will not be harmed or drown." I motioned to the people around the pool, encouraging her. "Look at everyone around here. You will be safe. Are you ready to show outwardly you accept Christ and you trust Him enough not only to save you, but to safely baptize you?"

After another 20–30 minutes of persuading, she agreed to be baptized. I dunked her back into the water, and when I lifted her back up, her face had entirely changed. Everyone around was shocked. She was no longer the same girl, gloomy with fear. Her face had peace.

I asked her, "Are you afraid now?"

""No," she said, smiling.

When a person receives water baptism, it is not for healing. It is an outward sign of their salvation. Healing comes with prayer, but here it was the commitment and decision she had made that delivered her from the spirits of fear. I am reminded of the verse from 1 John 4:18 that says "…the one who fears is not made perfect in love."

I am not talking about a mild fear. On Sunday, this girl was tormented by the enemy. She was a girl growing up without the love and care of a mother. She had a lot of responsibilities to her younger siblings and to her father. This was the main reason for her fear. Yet, when she came out of that water, she came out happy and at peace.

We prayed for her again and they went home to be a different family that day, free from fear and trauma. Sometimes people ask why I place so much importance on water baptism. You must realize that, especially in the Indian culture, there are people that worship a lot of gods. They have no problem accommodating Jesus as one more god among the many. But for sure, when one makes the decision publicly for Christ and walks publicly into the water at the time of baptism, it is not a mere teaching, but they experience the power of the true and living God through deliverance and healing. They come out of the water after baptism and there is no doubt left in their minds that Jesus is Lord and the only God they can trust.

Mark 16:16 (NIV) says, "Whoever believes and is baptized will be saved, but whoever does not believe will be condemned." They experience a renewed life with the death, burial, and resurrection of Christ, the real conversion. The enemy loses his grip on their soul, and they experience God's supernatural power and deliverance.

Time after time, I have seen breakthroughs after water baptism. Before the person is immersed in the water, they have one nature, but a completely new nature when they emerge from the water. Their lives have truly changed. When you frequently see these kinds of transformations, there is no reason left to doubt. I have had many occasions to baptize many people in my life. There have been times when it felt as if my only mission was to baptize people because of the visible transformations I encounter. A baptism isn't just some kind of religious symbolism, it is a powerful proclamation of our new life. In the case of this young lady, it was an act of war against the spirit of fear. By pushing back against the fear she felt, and allowing herself to be fully submitted to Christ, she showed that Lord Jesus had more power than fear. And for that, she was fully delivered.

Scripture References: Psalm 34:4; 1 John 4:18.

16.
SET FREE FROM RELIGIOUS BONDAGE

This story is about a baptism that took place in Karippuzha, in Alappuzha district, Kerala. We were at a house having an evening meeting where a young man in the family had recently received salvation. That evening I, along with a few other pastors, were worshiping and praying to the Lord and asking Him to bless the meeting. I had the opportunity to deliver the main message and the subject of my message was on the importance of salvation and water baptism.

At the end of my sermon, I gave an altar call. Several people came forward to accept Jesus Christ as their personal Savior and made the decision to be water baptized. Among them was an elderly lady who was about eighty-one years old.

She stood up and said, "I heard about water baptism, know about water baptism, and now I would like to be baptized."

It was evident by looking at her that physically she was too old to climb down to the pond—the water body that was used for baptism. She was weak and her hands shook as she walked. However, she was very clear in her mind and in her conviction, so we set a time and date for her baptism.

People came from all around to be baptized. At that time, baptisms took place wherever water was available, whether in a baptismal tank, a lake, or pond. We had workers who traveled the area, going from house to house to pray for the sick, and as a result many were healed, received salvation, and decided to be water baptized. It wasn't uncommon for us to have water baptisms three or more times in a single day. The day came for this elderly lady's baptism. She belonged to a family who were very devoted to the Marthoma Christian Church community. They believed that their church was indigenous and believed they carried the tradition from the Apostle Thomas of practicing little baby baptisms. Her sons' families, along with her grandchildren, were present during the baptism. She had the opportunity to be water baptized, along with her grandson. After her baptism, she said she wanted to testify.

"Forty-one years ago," she began, "I was convicted by the Word of God, that immersion baptism was right, but I was a part of a traditional and denominational Marthoma Christian church and did not want to come out of that. I disobeyed God's calling." It was a powerful opening. When we know what God tells us to do, but we choose to ignore it, we often struggle with regret. Clearly, she had never forgotten what God had told her to do, and it weighed on her.

"I have lived long enough to see my grandchildren growing up. When my grandson decided to be water baptized, I decided I could no longer hide the truth in me." With tears in her eyes, she said, "For forty-one years, I hid and disobeyed the truth. Today, I am eighty-one years old, and I don't want to wait any longer. I don't want to hide the truth and disobey the Holy Spirit."

I had baptized many people by that time, but I had never seen a person so joyous in being delivered from the bondages of religion and denominational traditions. She rejoiced in the Lord! Although some of her family remained in the denominational church, they all rejoiced along with this grandmother. I will never forget that day and how happy she was.

The Word of God is truth, and that truth has life—the eternal life! When someone experiences that truth, they will be set free of all sin and fear. Christianity is not a religion or a tradition or a denomination; it is a way of life! It is eternal life. This is one of the few occasions I felt so encouraged to do the Lord's work. The truth was with them, and the truth set them free!

Scripture References: Matthew 3:13–1; John 8:32, 34, 36; Romans 6:17–20; Ephesians 2:1–3, 1 John 2:3, 4:18.

17.
INFERTILITY HEALED

Linnet is my niece from Nilambur in Kerala, and she is a physiotherapist. A few years ago, she came to Pandalam, along with her cousins, Alice and Joy, to be water baptized. When she returned home after her baptism, her father, a strong denominational Orthodox Christian, was very angry and opposed her new life in Christ. She was raised to be married, and he did not want his daughter in a different denomination other than the Orthodox Church, much worse if Pentecostal.

Pentecostal Christians were and are viewed in Kerala with disdain. Being identified as a Pentecostal could make it hard for her to marry. He insisted that she would agree to an arranged marriage with a groom from the Orthodox Church community, and to please her father, she married a very handsome geologist. After they got married, they both took jobs in Bangalore.

A few years after her baptism, while I was visiting Wayanad, her father came from Nilambur to visit me. He had come for prayer because the family was going through a crisis. No one else but God could help, and during this difficult time, he was convinced to accept Christ and receive water baptism. He was willing to listen to the scriptures and accept the command of God because of what he was going through. The family's openness to the Word resulted in several miracles. It can be hard to understand how profound this was.

They were a part of the Orthodox Church and for them to accept a born-again, Pentecostal believer, or simply something other than their Orthodox tradition, it would subject them to ridicule and loss of status in the eyes of their community. It is a matter of pride. It is a form of religious bondage and a spirit of religion. It is a tradition carried forward from generation to generation. If someone leaves their denomination, they could get ridiculed and cut off, even within family members. It was a lot worse in those days, although things have improved in modern times with widespread access to the internet and publicity of ministries through online media.

When the father came for prayer, I wasn't going to offer a shallow prayer. I was going to share the truth of God's Word and my testimony and allow the Holy Spirit to speak to them. That is how a man who was adamant in his belief that only infants should be baptized found himself in a tank of water receiving baptism.

It was 10:00 a.m. when he was baptized. At the same time, Linnet and her husband heard about the revival meeting held in Wayanad, so they traveled from Bangalore that afternoon.

Linnet's husband was also like his father—stubborn and adamant about his orthodox denomination. We prayed with them when they arrived and around 2:00 p.m. that afternoon, her husband accepted Christ and was water baptized as well. He was ready to break the bondage to the religious denominational spirit.

What a remarkable thing! The father-in-law and the son-in-law—living in two different cities, both strong orthodox believers—accepting Christ and being water baptized on the same day in the same tank of water. The spirit of religion was broken in the family, setting them free from religion and drawing them to a relationship with our Savior.

We experience strong opposition and prejudice about certain doctrines or beliefs, but when God intervenes in someone's life, He can easily change their heart. After her husband's baptism, while we were still praying, Linnet said to me, "Uncle, we have been married for five years and we have no children. We had to undergo some treatments, but they didn't work. So would you please pray for us?"

During the meeting that night, many people came forward to pray, but Linnet and her husband didn't come, thinking they would be prayed for separately. It was midnight by the time the meeting ended. I forgot about needing to pray for Linnet. We said goodbye to everybody and climbed into the van. Suddenly, Linnet rushed to the van and said, "Uncle, you didn't pray for me!"

We climbed out of the vehicle and went into a room with her and her husband. We prayed a simple prayer for them, asking that God would give them a child. We left that night, and they all went to their own homes. I later heard through family that Linnet had moved to England for a job and the following year, they had a child. Now they all have migrated to England and live there, raising a family that a miracle of God provided.

God set them free from the spirit of religion and did an awesome miracle. He brought them closer to Him by demonstrating His love and compassion by delivering them from their bondages and physical infirmities.

HEALINGS AND DEMON POSSESSION

"For Jesus had said to him, 'Come out of this man, you evil spirit!'" (Mark 5:8).

When Paul speaks about the universe, he divides it into two groups: of this creation and not of this creation, otherwise, the visible creation and the invisible creation (Hebrews 9:11).

Angels and demons are not myths, they are reality, and their existence is a fact. *"For in Him all things were created, in heaven and on earth, visible and invisible, whether thrones or dominions or principalities or authorities—all things were created through him and for Him"* (Colossians 1:16).

Here, Paul speaks of the satanic world or the unseen demonic realm. Though invisible, they try to prompt and persuade human beings to go astray from the plan of God. Their role is to distract and keep humans preoccupied with many addictions, bondages, and emotional struggles, so that they can stay away from having an intimate relationship with God. Many people across the world falsely believe that these unseen spiritual entities are gods and are deceived into worshiping and being devoted to them. These entities then gain control over these people and control the way they think and act. People can be misled into being focused on their failures and remain in guilt, shame, and self-condemnation, thus missing the blessings and divine calling and purposes that God has planned for them.

Demonization is a slow process, as one gives into all these worldly temptations and falls into sin. One develops a chronic pattern that becomes a stronghold, a fortress of wrong thought processes, and robs them of their identity in who God created them to be. Satan has sent his demons to target both believers and unbelievers, as they have been watching us and know our weaknesses from our childhood, youth, and young adult life and also from generation to generation, as many weaknesses get passed on through the bloodline. They use humans against humans to divide, create strife and conflict, seduce and deceive, to lead them to his trap, into various bondages, bad habits, bad attitudes, chronic illnesses, and finally extreme demonization.

There are only two kingdoms—the Kingdom of Light, where Jesus Christ is King and the kingdom of darkness, ruled by the devil with the multitude of evil spirits.

These spirits invade the human soul, body, and mind and over a period of time take control of a lot of decision making, attitudes, and actions. Unbelievers can be easily controlled as they follow many occult and pagan practices that serve the purpose of these evil spirits. Believers in Christ, or traditional Christians, are impacted by demonic torment when they depart from Christian fellowship and intimacy with God through prayer and worship, becoming lukewarm. The evil spirits consistently lead them into temptation and failure in many aspects of their lives, depriving them of God's blessings, anointing, and fruitfulness.

In this book you will read some of the ways during my youth and how I drifted away from the path of a godly life to becoming a rebel, getting into addictions and bondage, then running away from home to live a destructive life on the streets, homeless and separated from home and family. But God had mercy on me and returned me back to Him and His ways to live a life in the fulness of His blessings.

But there is deliverance for anyone who wants to be set

free. For those who want to repent, turn away from their sinful actions and renounce those addictions, bondages, and bad attitudes. The evil spirits that torment humanity can be cast out in the mighty name of Jesus Christ, because He is the Creator and Ruler of the visible and invisible worlds. He is the Preserver and Governor of all things. All spiritual entities are subject to Him and must bow down to His authority.

"Having disarmed principalities and powers, He made a public spectacle of them, triumphing over them in it" (Colossians 2:15).

As ministers of the gospel, we confront these spirits while ministering, but we must know that Jesus gave His followers the unquestionable authority to cast these spirits out. For doing that, we need the anointing of the Holy Spirit, which is the Spirit of Light. When the Spirit of Light comes forth, then the spirit of darkness must flee.

Jesus said, *"The thief comes only to steal, kill and destroy; I have come that they may have life, and have it to the full" (John 10:10).*

Through Jesus Christ, we can have that wholesome, fruitful, and fulfilled life in abundance. He has authority over all forces on earth and in the heavens, in the seen and unseen realms.

In Matthew 28:18 at the beginning of His great commission discourse, Jesus said, *"All authority in heaven and on earth has been given to Me."*

In Mark 16:17 Jesus said, *"And these signs will accompany those who believe: In My name they will drive out demons."* Yes, Jesus Christ has given believers the authority by the Holy Spirit to command and drive out and evict demons who oppress, harass, and disrupt people's lives.

"Therefore God exalted Him to the highest place and gave

Him the name that is above every name, that at the name of Jesus, every knee should bow, in heaven and on earth and under the earth, and every tongue acknowledge that Jesus Christ is Lord, to the glory of God the Father" (Philippians 2:9–10).

18.
A MAN WITH KIDNEY DISEASE HEALED

In the early days of our ministry, especially in my hometown, Pandalam, we had no place to worship or even stay, so whenever I went there, I stayed at the only hotel in town. Many people would come see me for prayer for their physical or material needs. In the beginning, I had no specific plan of what to do other than to obey God's call to "go back to my people." Most of the time, we met with some local pastors for prayer and to minister to them. I talked to everyone who came about the good news of God and His power to deliver people.

One evening, a thirty-four-year-old man and his wife came to visit me. He was tall, slim, and could barely walk because he was so weak. He was only able to take small steps while leaning on his wife. They sat down in my room to talk to me. "Somebody told us you are in healthcare," he said. "I wanted to show you what the doctors are saying." His wife handed me a bundle of medical records that spanned the previous 10–12 years.

I quickly scanned the medical records and doctors' notes from Trivandrum and Kottayam medical colleges and found that he was diagnosed with pyelonephritis, a condition affecting his kidneys. I asked more questions about their background and where they were from. They were of a Hindu background and very poor. He had a job in a restaurant as a cook. They had two children. He was being treated in many different hospitals. The wife's family had given them some financial help for his treatment, but they could no longer afford to help. They were not looking for prayer or any spiritual help, but for financial support.

I gave them some money, and then I started speaking to them about Jesus Christ. I shared how God intervened in my life and healed me. Finally, I prayed for them, and they appeared to be content with the small amount of money I was able to give them. Before they left, I told them about the meeting to be held the next evening in the conference hall of the local Marthoma Church Centre.

The next morning, things went as usual and, in the evening, we had a deliverance meeting. I was still very new to the ministry in those days, so Pastor Peter and I invited special guests for our various meetings around the community. Pastor Raju from Kottayam, a man anointed to cast out evil spirits, was among the teachers there. It was a wonderful service, and I was pleased with the attendance. Everyone sat on the floor on mats and listened to the message. During and after the meeting, we called for special prayers.

Many people came forward for prayer. The man who visited me the previous night was sitting on the floor in the corner of the auditorium, backed up to the wall and listening to the message. I noticed he was able to walk by himself, which was an improvement over the previous day.

As we went from one person to another, we laid our hands on his head and we prayed. Suddenly, this weak man started moving violently, raising his hands, and pushing everybody out. He started rolling and moving his hands and legs ferociously and he became violent. Seven people who stood near him struggled to hold him down, but they could not control him. He threw things out, kicking and hitting people madly. The previous night, he could barely walk or stand up without help, so we knew this was not his strength. He was possessed by an evil spirit, and the spirit started to manifest in the presence of worship and the name of Jesus Christ.

Some of the believers gathered were very familiar with this kind of behavior and they responded. Seven men stood around him and held him tight to the floor. Yet, he was struggling to throw them all off. Then, when Pastor Raju came forward and confronted the evil spirit, it started to speak by chanting some Islamic prayer and showing different gestures and rolling his eyes.

The spirit that possessed him was sent by a Muslim mullah to bind him up and to kill him gradually—a form of witchcraft. The spirit said there was a woman behind this act. She had loved him fourteen years ago and was willing to marry him, but he married another woman. This provoked her to try to destroy their married life and to kill him. He had been tormented by this spirit in different forms of sickness—finally, the doctors gave a diagnosis to it by calling it a "kidney disease" for the last fourteen years.

Pastor Raju commanded the evil spirit in the name of Jesus Christ to obey and to come out of the man. The man acted violently and the spirit inside him spoke, saying, "I am not alone but many. We tried to put the disease on him."

While he had been possessed, the evil spirit claimed his name to be "Jinn." Then, though he was Hindu, he began to sing an Islamic devotional song far better than a Muslim mullah would. This showed that it was a real spirit because a Hindu man had no reason to know a Muslim devotional song.

The man started moving his arms over his own body and when he came to both sides of the flank where the kidneys are located, he began to make a motion as if he were pulling something out.

It didn't stop there, so we continued for some time with

prayer and taking authority. Then we saw a miraculous act of the Spirit of God. After a while, this man came to his senses and the evil spirit left him. When he came to himself, we asked him how he felt, and he said he was all right. He felt like the sickness was gone and, though still weak, he left the meeting that night in his own strength. The next morning, I baptized the couple in a small tank of water at my father's house.

I was told that jinn is a kind of evil spirit, usually sent out by a Muslim sorcerer or magician.

They claim that jinns are very powerful and that it is very difficult to cast them out. Yet, with God all things are possible, and in the name of Jesus Christ, every demonic spirit will flee. God can use His elect to exercise His authority over these spirits. That doesn't mean that we are superhuman, but we are ordinary people cleansed by the blood of Jesus Christ and anointed by the Holy Spirit to do His works.

I was amazed to see the so-called powerful spirit trembling and screaming with fear and agony in the holy congregation. Yes, the wicked one cannot stand in the assembly of the saints. After witnessing this deliverance, my own understanding of faith and the power in the name of Jesus Christ increased significantly.

Afterwards, that man became a Christian. Some non-Christian fanatics approached him and told him they would kill him if he continued to practice Christianity. However, according to the last report I received, he and his wife continue to serve the Lord Jesus Christ.

Scripture References: John 10:10; Mark 5:8, Matthew 8:28–34; Luke 8:18–39.

19.
GIRL WITH CHRONIC HEADACHES DELIVERED FROM DEMONIC POSSESSION

Late one Friday evening, we arrived at the Sultan Bathery mission field in the Wayanad district of Northern Kerala after a grueling twelve-hour trip over bad roads. We were anxious to get to bed, but when we arrived, there was a group waiting for us to pray. Our team consisted of a couple of pastors from Pandalam, including Pastor Peter and Pastor Raju, who I mentioned in another story. These men had a special anointing to cast out demons.

We conducted a short meeting where we worshiped and shared a short message. After the message, we gave the congregants an opportunity to come forward for special prayers. Many left, but a few stayed back for the prayer. One of them was a neighbor and a friend of the pastor, who was a businessman and a local politician. He, his wife, son, and daughter were all Hindu devotees.

He brought his fifteen-year-old daughter forward, a very talented and beautiful girl who suffered from chronic headaches. They were so severe that she could no longer concentrate on her studies. She was an award winner in Bharath Natyam, an ancient classical dance from southern India, usually performed by one dancer and based on Hindu mythology.

The dance movements of the hands and arms have an elaborate and stylized symbolic meaning. According to tradition, these dances originate from gods and goddesses of dance. The ones who partake in these dances could be spiritually bonded with those gods.

Her parents were very concerned by the frequency and severity of the headaches, as well as the impact these attacks were having on her studies. We all sat down to pray and worship the Lord for a bit and then the host pastor led us in laying our hands on this young girl to pray for deliverance from the headaches. The parents and many others were standing by watching when suddenly, she started showing signs of demonic manifestation. Then she fell on the floor and started rolling.

Demon spirits started showing themselves by screaming, moving her extremities violently, sticking her tongue out, rolling her eyes back, tearing at her clothes, and pulling her hair. So Pastor Raju began to question the spirit.

At first, it was reluctant to speak the truth and made many mumbling noises and refused to answer. When the worship started, the spirits became restless and agitated and started reluctantly to reveal information by different signs or words.

We could recognize the spirits by the revealing signs and sounds. These images are presently engraved in the temples as gods and goddesses being worshiped by these Hindu devotees. The names of these spirits were very familiar to the parents and the people sitting around because they were the deities they worshiped, but these were the spirits causing the sickness and destruction of this young girl.

While Pastor Raju was encountering the possessed girl, we all started to worship, pray, and praise God in a spirit-filled way by speaking in tongues and rebuking the spirit. Some of us were quoting verses from the Bible, and we all were strengthened by the godly authority of the Holy Spirit. The powerful worship forced the evil spirits to obey the command. They surrendered to the name of Jesus and agreed to leave her. Many hours passed and as each demon left, they took their sickness and infirmities with them.

This is the reality. Even though this family worshiped these spirits as gods, they didn't have the character of the true God. Instead, they were destructive and punishing spirits that were destroying this girl for their pleasure. The demons possessing this young girl were supposed to be goddesses. When we began to rebuke them in Jesus Christ's name and authority, they manifested and showed their true character. The facial expressions and things they did were familiar to the people there because they were the movements of the goddess they worshiped. The people offer sacrifices to these deities to protect the worshipers from harm, but, in fact, their worship of these deities brought them harm.

Galatians 4:8 says, "Formerly, when you did not know God, you were slaves to those who by nature are not gods." The true God has his own nature—compassion and love—but these gods are cruel by nature. They don't have the nature of God in them, but they are called gods and goddesses by people who submit and bow down to them.

The biggest controversy is when we call a spirit a "demon" when others call them "gods." That is where a lot of enmity comes between the people who worship these gods and true worshipers of the living God. We are preaching the opposite of what they believe, and they don't want to hear that they are worshiping the wrong ones. So we are careful to share the truth with them in love.

I want to share a few more details of what happened so you understand the authority you have. When the demons manifested themselves, sometimes the girl got up and did the dances she was known for. Among them was the goddess of dance, who is seen in images with her tongue hanging out. While the pastor was praying over the girl, at one point her eyes became red. The families noticed it but were more focused on the demons coming out of her. The pastor said to the demons, "Whoever put this redness in her eye, take it out right now in Jesus' name!" As soon as he said that, the girl wiped her eye with her hand, and the redness went away.

Finally, about four hours later, five kinds of demonic spirits came out of her. She came to herself, and she started to speak normally. She asked for a drink of water and sat up with everybody, as she was feeling fine. She was quite relieved. The demons had left her.

During this event, I noticed a few things that have remained in my memory. The possessed girl was acting violently and had superhuman strength. She was trying to attack and hit people, but the pastor simply commanded the spirits to calm down. He said, "You cannot move your hands until I say you can." And it was so; she couldn't move that hand, as he had bound it in the spirit. He was speaking in the authority of the word of God and in the name of Jesus Christ.

The Bible describes how believers have authority over evil spirits. If you command them in the name of Jesus Christ, they must obey. For almost half an hour, the girl could not move her hands—as if they were nailed to the ground. Once she was delivered and started behaving normally, the pastor said she could move her hands and she then began to move her hands around. There was no visible sign of any kind of pressure or force, but it was only by the manifestation of the Word that her hands were kept from moving. This was something new to me, and I was totally amazed.

Her father cried as he sat beside her and watched everything unfold. He himself seemed to be receiving deliverance as the demons were leaving his daughter. His hardened heart was touched by the power and compassion of Jesus Christ. Meanwhile, the girl's mother was slithering on the floor on her belly like a snake and dancing around. She had also been delivered after those manifestations.

Finally, after watching the demonstration of the power of God and all these evil spirits, her father stood up and said:

"I have been a Hindu all through my life. I always respected all the gods and even Jesus Christ, as I considered Him as one of the gods. But today I have seen and experienced something different. Jesus Christ is the only God, and no other gods have power like Jesus. No one else has authority like Jesus, no one else has compassion like Jesus and no one else has healing power like Jesus."

He continued to say, "From today onwards, I want to believe in Jesus Christ fully and obey His commandments. I don't just want to be an average Christian. I am going to practice Christianity as the Bible says."

On that day, the father, his wife, and two grown-up children, including the girl, decided to receive Christ as their personal Savior and to be water baptized. Along with them, five other young people who witnessed the entire event of deliverance accepted Christ as their personal Savior and decided to be water baptized.

That morning, we took nine people to the lake, but this incident paved the way to establishing a church in that place. We experienced many new and mightier experiences like this in that area thereafter, too. The church grew to be a very strong, full-fledged church and a lot of believers were added and continue to attend there to this day. In fact, two of the people baptized that day now serve the Lord in full-time ministry.

The girl, who was once possessed by demons, got delivered by Jesus Christ and then went on to pursue education and successfully graduated as a professional nurse. Her father later became a political and influential leader in that region.

Even though it has been many years since that happened, I still remember the story as if it were happening before me right now.

Scripture References: Luke 9:1; Matthew 28:18, 19; Mark 1:17; Matthew 8:8–34; Luke 8:38–39.

20.
THE SUICIDAL MAN
SET FREE

We had another mission to Sultan Bathery, which is a twelve-hour trip by train and bus from Pandalam. Because we already had participated in several back-to-back programs in different places that day, we were hungry and exhausted, so when we got on the train, all we wanted was some food and rest. Unfortunately, that led to me eating way too much food from the vendors on the train, and I got sick. To make matters worse, once we arrived in the northern Kerala city of Calicut, we transferred to a bus, but someone stole my wallet with my identification, credit cards, and some of my cash.

Only after reaching Sultan Bathery, were we able to have some warm food, which helped a little, but I was physically and psychologically exhausted when we arrived at the house where we were to stay at. When we reached the house, several people were waiting for prayer. Despite my own physical limitations, we had a tremendous service that went well into the night. We didn't get to bed until the early dawn hours, but it was worth it. We had many deliverances and healings that night. We only slept a few hours before people began coming again for prayer to the house.

One young man in his early thirties stands out in my memory. Somebody brought him for prayer because he had attempted suicide. The spirit of suicide was controlling his life, and he no longer wanted to live. When he arrived at the house, I was still in my room, so the other pastors greeted him in the living room and began talking to him.

As they continued to talk to him, we found out that his wife was in the hospital having their first child. Why would he want to die during such a happy time? He said he had been unfaithful to his wife during her pregnancy and felt unworthy of seeing his child. He wanted to die before the child was born, so he had made up his mind to commit suicide.

Everybody tried to convince him that he didn't have to die. God could forgive him, cleanse him, and restore his life. He didn't want to be comforted. His guilt was too intense, and he was unwilling to ask for or to receive forgiveness. Sometimes people want to punish themselves with the pain of guilt and self-condemnation, and that was what this man was doing.

"Will you pray for him?" one of the pastors asked. I raised a hand and closed my eyes to pray for him and as soon as I did, this man fell face down on the concrete floor. We hadn't even physically touched him. We hadn't even begun the prayer.

The other pastors were in a panic. "Don't worry," I said. "Leave him alone. Let him be there. Don't help him up."

He was there for about 15–20 minutes, lying on the floor without any movement. After twenty minutes, he opened his eyes and got up and he started crying out saying, "I don't want to die! I don't want to go to the place I just saw!" Later, he would tell us of the horror he saw and experienced during those twenty minutes of terrible darkness, fear, and oppression. He had seen hell.

He wanted to change his life. I told him, "Only Jesus can change your life. "Accept Him as your Lord and Savior and let Him wash you clean." He accepted Jesus Christ and God washed away all his sins and guilt. We immediately took him to the water and baptized him.

Had that man walked out the door that day, we would not have been able to do anything for him. He was lost, but God had other plans. When he fell on the floor, God was intervening in his life. After receiving baptism, he felt an immense peace, which he had never felt in his life before. He had experienced the deliverance from bondage and death to freedom in Christ.

That day, after we prayed for him to have a complete deliverance, he went to the hospital. That night, his wife gave birth to their first child. Their life totally changed, and they became faithful members of the church, and now they serve the Lord as a family.

Only God can cause an amazing story like this. What a wonderful Lord we serve! What a wonderful Savior we have! Jesus Christ can deliver us from all kinds of evil and death. We are very happy we could help this young man, not only by saving his life, but by restoring his family.

My mission trips are grueling, but whenever I see these kinds of deliverances, I forget all my fatigue and all the work. Despite my own frustrations that day, all fatigue and discomfort disappeared when I experienced what God had planned and orchestrated. As with so many of these stories, the miracle led to the establishment of a church in that area. We started the Kuppady church in Wayanad. Later, we would establish many churches around it.

While there may be trials as you walk out God's call, you will also experience great victories that restore all you have lost, just like the people you pray for.

21.
A BLIND WOMAN HEALED

During one of our trips to Wayanad, we met Bhaskaran, whose daughter was delivered by prayer on our previous trip. He asked us to go pray for a blind woman in the village of Puthupappady. It is about 25–30 miles deep into the forest, away from the town of Sultan Bathery. Even though it was late in the evening and the trip would take a couple of hours, because of the urgent request we agreed to go there. This was a denominational Christian family who had invited many of their friends and relatives for prayer that evening. Pastor Peter, Pastor Achankunju, and some new believers from the Kuppady church accompanied us. Because there were so many people waiting for us, we held an evening worship service. I delivered a short message from John 10:10, which says, *"The thief comes only to* steal and kill and destroy; I have come that they may have *life and have it to the full"* (emphasis mine). I also shared my testimony with them of how God healed my blinded eye.

At the end, when we gave an invitation to accept Christ, many accepted. After we prayed for everyone and while we were preparing to come back, we realized that although we went to pray for the blind woman, we ended up praying for everyone else except her. She was a very nice, middle-aged woman sitting in the corner, not verbalizing any complaints. She had lost her vision over four and a half years earlier, apparently for no documented reason. She was treated by many local physicians without any cure. Later, I was told she had surgery on her eyes at a medical college, which made her vision worse until gradually she became totally blind. She was also getting weaker, and she could not even walk around. She sat on the floor and scooted around the house in total blindness.

So we went to her because we weren't going to end without doing what we came for. We laid our hands on her and prayed for her healing. The moment we laid our hands on her head and started worshiping and praying, she began to suddenly move her arms violently and shake her body. She nearly fell to the ground. Those who knew her said that they had never seen her do that before.

We started to sense an evil spirit manifesting in her. So we started to pray in the Holy Spirit, speaking in tongues and worshiping God. While we were worshiping, the demonic spirit started to speak. We questioned this evil spirit in the name of Jesus because we stood firm and took authority in His name. The manifestation of the spirit became very intense, and it started revealing so many events in the family and how it possessed this woman. The spirit also revealed its name as Kaalan, which was supposed to be the spirit of death, known to be a stubborn and a very powerful spirit to cast out. With strong worship and commanding in the name of Jesus, this spirit started to tremble and say, "It is very hot. I am very thirsty. Give me milk to drink. I cannot stay here; give me all my demands and I will leave." The demand was to pay off the sorcerer with 20,000 rupees.

It had been a family member that bound the spirit on her to inherit her family's wealth after her premature death. The conversation with this evil spirit lasted over an hour, and we commanded it in the name of Jesus to leave her without any of its demands. After that, the woman came to her senses. We opened the Bible and asked her to read something. She sat there and read one whole paragraph from the Bible. Despite four and a half years of blindness, she could now see things normally. Her immediate deliverance amazed many who gathered there. Many who stood around to see this manifestation of the deceptive spirit understood the power of God and many more believed in that town.

By this supernatural deliverance, one more unreached village heard the good news of the gospel, more captives were set free, and another blind person started to see the light. Isaiah 61:1 says, "He has sent me to bind up the brokenhearted, to proclaim freedom for the captives and release from darkness for the prisoners."

Some may question why we speak with an evil spirit. Some ask, "Why can't you just cast it out in Jesus' name? Why do the evil spirits come to Christians?" These questions have been raised many times, even by Christian ministers. When we see these kinds of powerful deliverances, we cannot deny the power of the enemy to cause all sorts of sickness and problems. The manifestations of these spirits vary from person to person, and it is important that we are led by the anointing of the Holy Spirit to ensure total freedom to the oppressed individual. Fear has no place in these encounters and often time is not a constraint in deliverances. Our goal is to set the individual free, completely, and help them gain understanding as to why this has occurred in the first place. The rest of the theological and doctrinal questions raised are not necessarily of importance in short services and public meeting ministries. Long-term care and further education from God's Word are provided once the individual is ready to learn and progress in their faith and allow the Holy Spirit to bring the transformation and full deliverance and inner healing.

I had never seen blindness due to demon possession before this incident. We can't underestimate what the enemy can do. In this encounter with the demonic, the deceptive spirit was exposed for his destructive purpose and for stealing the well-being of the people. When people witness this and see this kind of demonstration of the power of God, it is much easier to witness and have them receive Jesus Christ.

"Then they brought Him a demon-possessed man who was blind and mute, and Jesus healed Him, so that He could both talk and see" (Matthew 12:22). Yes, demons can cause one to be blind and mute and much more. But the power of Jesus Christ can set anyone free from years of blindness or muteness and any other such physical infirmities.

22.
DELIVERED FROM ALCOHOLISM AND SUICIDE

In the early days of our ministry, we established a church in the southern Indian metro city of Bangalore in Karnataka state in a slum area called Ulsoor. Most of the people in that area live in tents without running water, clothes, or basic hygiene. Many of them work for the municipality as scavengers, cleaning the drainage systems or the public toilets. It is a very sad place full of hopelessness, but this is where the Lord led us to start a ministry, and later, our first church.

On one of my early trips to that area, I was walking with a pastor on the street. Suddenly, a man started running towards us, and when he came close by, he fell at my feet, crying. We lifted him up, and he started telling the story of the last six months of his life. At that time, he lived in the slum area of Ulsoor. He was a very poor Hindu man who spoke Tamil.

He had a business of selling vegetables door-to-door in a little, open cart. He was supporting his family and small children with that business; however, he became an alcoholic and all the money he made went for drinking and other wasteful activities. He could not support his family anymore because he couldn't seem to remain sober. In his depressed thinking, there was nothing left for him and for his family. He was in debt and a huge amount of it had to be paid to many people and money lenders. He felt there was no other option but to commit suicide.

One day, he bought some poison to drink with the plan to end his life that day. But he happened to meet with our pastor, Johnny, who led him to Christ. This poor Hindu who felt there was nothing more to live for accepted this unheard-of God and received Jesus Christ into his heart as his personal Savior. His life changed, and he became a different man.

He stopped drinking and turned his focus back to making his business successful, eventually paying off all his debts. In fact, the debts that felt so large that he thought death was his only option were actually paid off within six months! He and his family started attending church regularly, and he started obeying by tithing his income. The change in him was not internal or spiritual alone—it was visible to others. People saw that the God he believed in had radically changed his life. Many people in that slum area came to the knowledge of Christ and within a short time, we started a church in the slums of Ulsoor.

When he saw us on the street, his heart was filled with gratitude towards the God who saved him and the people who brought him to that experience. That is why he fell to the ground, thanking God for what He had done in his life.

Here we see the life-changing experience that no other God but Jesus Christ offered to this man. Because of that man, salvation has come to many others, and the church was established in that area. Because of one man's faithfulness, God did wonders and miracles for many in that area and brought that village to salvation in Jesus Christ.

SIGNS AND WONDERS

"He got up, rebuked the wind and said to the waves,
'Quiet! Be still!' Then the wind died down and it was
completely calm" (Mark 4:39).

God can do wonderful things not only in human beings, but He can control nature and seasons for the wellbeing of his elect ones and sometimes to demonstrate His power and specific purposes for a region or a nation.

Throughout the Bible, we see how God shows who He is through signs and wonders.

Apostle Paul wrote in Romans 1:20, "For since the creation of the world, God's invisible qualities—His eternal power and divine nature have been clearly seen, being understood from what has been made so that people are without excuse."

God has set some rules over this universal system to operate according to His plan from creation, which we call natural laws. The course of natural laws typically flows without a break and has been well understood and researched by scientists throughout history. But if that natural flow is broken, we call it a miracle.

Such miracles were not only seen in the gospels, where Jesus performed many signs, wonders, and miracles. Many such signs and wonders can be seen throughout the scriptures, where God demonstrated His power through many of His chosen prophets and servants.

In one such miracle, we read in the Old Testament that when Joshua commanded the army of Israel, the traffic system of the whole universe stopped for a day. The sun stood still in the sky while the battle for the Promised Land raged on, bringing victory for God's people.

Another miracle happened when Elijah prayed for the heavens to close for three years. There was no rain, but when he prayed again, it rained. The heavy downpour was mighty enough to stop the royal chariots. The God who did these things in the Bible is the same God today. In the following pages, you will read how God intervened in our natural system to perform wonderful miracles for His people.

We read about all the great signs and wonders God demonstrated through His servant Moses in Egypt, in the process of setting His chosen people free from being slaves to that nation to become a chosen nation—God's own.

God is still working such miracles, even today. He demonstrates His love and compassion for humanity through these signs, so that all men can draw near to Him.

23.
BREAKING THE CHAIN
OF POVERTY

Pastor Joy lived in a small, one-room apartment in Dharavi, in the heart of the mega metro city of Mumbai. In those days, Dharavi was the largest slum in all of Asia. It is a very uncomfortable place for an outsider to walk through because of the stench from the open sewer and strewn garbage. Housing in Mumbai is very expensive and very scarce, so Pastor Joy had to live in that area despite all the inconveniences. He lived there with his wife, two children, and mother-in-law in that small apartment. In my early ministry days, on one of my many trips to Mumbai, Pastor Joy had met me at the Mumbai railway station. I had met him once before in Kerala, as his wife was from my hometown. Pastor Joy's only profession was to go around and give gospel tracts, witness about Jesus Christ, and pray for people. His only livelihood was the little amount of money he received as an offering for his ministry to people he visited, as he didn't have a regular church or congregation.

During that visit, he invited me to his home to share a meal with his family and I obliged. The family was gracious, and since I was from Pandalam, his wife was looking forward to cooking me some food like that from our hometown. Usually, I would not have been able to eat in the area because I wasn't used to such a foul smell in the air, but on this occasion, I gladly dined with them.

After lunch, we all gathered to pray. My heart was broken

to see the condition they were living in. The house was also not large enough to accommodate the family and was in a very unhealthy place. I prayed earnestly for God to change their situation. My prayer was that the Lord would move them out of that slum and bless him with a better place to live and to raise his children. I said to the Lord, "Lord, he is your servant and doesn't know any other job besides serving you."

After that visit, I would occasionally send him financial help because he did not have his own income. I cried and prayed, "Don't make this man live here anymore!" When I cried out, they also cried together with me.

I gave them some money to buy clothes or books for the children and some household belongings, then I left. That year, somehow, the Lord helped me to sponsor him to come to America. I have attempted to sponsor many pastors like this, but many of them were not able to get approval from immigration for travel.

When Pastor Joy applied for a visa, they issued him a sixty-day visa, although typically pastors get visas for three to six months. Despite the small disappointment, we were overjoyed he was able to come. He came and spent fifty-nine days in America, visiting some friends, well-wishers, and churches. The Lord was with him during his entire trip, and he left before the visa expired.

People from church communities helped him financially, and through that support, he had more than enough to pay off all the debts he had and to build a new house for his family. In later years, he ended up getting a visa for ten years and has visited America often.

This is one example of God answering prayers to break the chain of poverty. God blessed this family and enabled them to achieve greater things in life. Because Pastor Joy served

God, He did not leave him in that slum long and delivered him and his family. What a wonderful testimony of the faithfulness of God.

During that first visit to his home in Mumbai, he had volunteered to take me around to pray with the people he saw regularly in his ministry. One of the people he visited regularly was a retired railway officer who was paralyzed and homebound because of a stroke. The man needed assistance to get up because he was paralyzed on the right side. When he heard I was visiting, he wanted me to come and visit for prayer. Whenever I visit a patient, I tell my story of how God miraculously healed me from various illnesses and healed my blinded eye when there was no other treatment available to me. So, as usual, I shared my healing testimony and what the Lord had done in my life with this man. I shared my testimony quickly, and we prayed. I raised my hand, praying for him, and then I lifted his paralyzed hand, and he began to praise God with me. I let go but told him to keep his hand up. He did. He could not do that before. God healed him instantly. There in Mumbai, I witnessed one more of God's miraculous healings, for the glory of God.

.Scripture References: Mark 2:2–12; Matthew 9:2–8; Luke 5:18–25.

24.
A CRIMINAL BECOMES AN EVANGELIST

I was first told of this story by one of our pastors. This incident happened in the small town of Rahuri, in Ahmednagar district of Maharashtra. Later, I met the man they spoke about in person and had the opportunity to hear him testify as well. It is truly a remarkable thing and shows the power of redemption God has for those willing to be used for His glory.

One of our native missionaries went to a home in the village to pray. That area was very dangerous for Christians and missionaries because of the anti-Christian fanatics opposed to our work. I have been told that in this area, churches were burned and mission workers were brutally attacked. The pastor in this story, however, was from that area, so he was able to move among the people. His recognition in the area, as well as divine protection, is the only explanation I have for his ability to minister so freely in such a dangerous area.

On one occasion, he went to a home where a woman and her children were living. After giving her some gospel literature, he offered to pray for them. The woman turned to him in disgust and asked him, "What prayer? My husband has been in prison for the last eight and a half years and we have been left alone. No prayer can change our condition. If my husband comes back or if your God can let him out of prison, then I will believe in your prayers and in your God."

That was quite a challenge. Her husband had been convicted of murder and was sentenced to life in prison at one of the central jails and could not be released. So the pastor did what he could; he just prayed and went away without convincing them.

Three days after the pastor's visit, the imprisoned man was standing in front of their house, to the complete shock of his family. He came home straight away from the prison. Nobody knows how it happened, but he was released after serving only eight and a half years because of some technicality. The reason didn't matter to this woman because all she knew was that her husband, a murderer serving a life sentence, had been released from prison by God's power.

Soon after he arrived home, his wife told him about the pastor and about his prayer. He, of course, wanted to find this pastor to ask what had happened. The pastor was called back to the house, and he spent some time with the family. He shared the gospel with the family, and as they listened, they were convinced that Christ could deliver those who pray to Him. On that day, the whole family, including the ex-prisoner, accepted Jesus Christ as their personal Lord and personal Savior. This news spread all over the village.

The salvation of this convicted murderer completely changed people's opinion of Christianity. News of this miraculous deliverance spread throughout the village quickly. Since that time, he has also begun to work with us by helping protect those going into dangerous areas to share the gospel. He is a very tall and physically imposing man, so he used to accompany the pastor because once people saw this man, nobody opposed him. His reputation as a well-known criminal in that village, as well as his imposing body size, offered additional physical protection.

After I heard the story, I made it a point to meet this man on my next trip to Maharashtra. I heard his testimony of what had happened to him, and we took some pictures together.

Now we have churches in that village, and that village was totally evangelized through this one man's conversion.

While it is easy to recognize healing miracles, this is a different kind of miracle! A criminal was absolutely changed and became a servant of God, serving Christ daily after being released from a life sentence. What a wonderful, life-changing story! It is amazing how God used the bravery of one pastor to pray with a hurt and angry woman and to continue praying even after he left her home, which opened the door to the miraculous.

I pray that we all understand the power of God. Is there anything too hard for our Lord? In Jeremiah 32:27 it says, "I am the Lord the God of all mankind. Is anything too *hard for me?*" There is absolutely nothing too hard for our Lord.

Scripture References: Corinthians 5:17; Psalm 40:3; Ezekiel 36:26.

25.
STORY OF MY
LAST RUPEE

During the transition phase, when I was a runaway, homeless and living on the streets or in temporary accommodations for over two years, I was in Kankanady, Mangalore in 1963. I was just starting the paramedical training program with Swiss Emmaus at Father Muller's hospital. In this program, we had one month of training and then an exam. We were not paid during this time, but if we passed the entrance exam, we could enter the full program where we would receive a stipend. I had passed the first part and was beginning the second month of training, so it would be another two weeks before I received any stipends or salary. By this point, I'd used up all the money I had earned previously by working at a restaurant, and I was down to the last rupee in my pocket.

My roommate and I were leaving our room to get breakfast before classes that day. Almost immediately after I walked out our door, I heard a child's footsteps. When I turned around, it was my neighbor's son asking for a rupee for them to buy some food for her children. I took the rupee out of my pocket and gladly gave it to him without thinking about it. He turned around and ran back to his home.

Almost immediately, the reality of what I had done struck me. That was my last rupee. During this time, I was not a believer. In fact, I had run away from home in disgrace two years earlier and never told my parents where I was going or where I currently was. My life was only focused on eating, smoking cigarettes, and going to my classes. Now I had no money to do two of those three things.

I wasn't sure what to do, but my roommate and I continued to the coffee shop for breakfast and then went on to class. There was no other way of getting any money now, although I'd get sixty rupees in a couple of weeks. I didn't worry about what I would do, focusing instead on going to my class.

During that day before lunch break, the postman was looking for me. He had a money order for fifty rupees for me. I was so excited I didn't even ask where it was from. I had not had anyone send me money for over two years, but I received it the day I needed it. In fact, that was enough money to carry me until I received my first stipend check. It was many years later that I learned that my roommate had contacted my parents to tell them I was doing okay and where I was. They had sent the money to me, without my knowledge, and it arrived just in time when I needed it.

This is the goodness of God. Not only did He provide for my need for money, but He provided my parents with the reassurance that I was safe. I did not know God's will at that time, but His caring for me in my time of need was a miracle.

26.
OUT OF BODY EXPERIENCE

In 2009, I had just returned to Houston from a six-week trip to India when I was told that my younger brother had a heart attack. So I went to visit him at his home. My heart ached when I saw how sick he was and that I had not been available for him at the time of his critical need. Later, I found out also that my neighbor had a heart attack and was in the hospital at that time, so I visited him as well. Both these people were younger than me, and while I've had chest pains on occasions, I was always fine.

Around that time, one night after a very nice seafood dinner, I went to bed about 4:00 a.m. and woke up not long after feeling very uncomfortable with an upset stomach. I was so sick that I began to wonder if I had food poisoning. I was beginning to sweat and nearly collapsed, so Susie was worried, and she called our children. My son-in-law, Roy, rushed to our house to check on me and called the ambulance. When the paramedics arrived, they hooked me up to IVs and oxygen. It was confusing and overwhelming feeling so sick and having so much happening around me. My blood pressure had dropped very low, so they transported me to the hospital, and Susie followed behind with some of our family.

A team of doctors and nurses, including a cardiologist, were waiting for me at the emergency room while I was still on the stretcher. I was moved to an assigned room, and they continued to do related emergency procedures on me.

"He is having a severe heart attack," I heard the cardiologist say.

I remember I was calling upon the name of the Lord Jesus Christ, and the next thing I remember was that I felt a bright light around me, and I was taken to a large open place that was very peaceful. I knew that I felt the presence of the Lord Jesus, who I was calling upon, in that very open place. He assured me, and I found extreme peace and comfort. I was free from pain and fear. I was somehow aware that the doctors and nurses were working on me, and my family was all around me as well and praying that I was going to be okay. When I came back to my physical awareness, I realized that I was still in the emergency room. But I couldn't feel the severeness of the heart attack's impact on my body. My family was continuously praying and trusting in God during that time, and my heart condition gradually improved.

I was admitted to the ICU for several days before transferring to Saint Luke's Hospital Cardiac Institute, where I had to undergo surgery for a coronary blockage. I recovered and came home. When I realized I was in the emergency room having a heart attack and experiencing severe pain, I called on Jesus. He took my soul away from that dark moment of pain and distress, and He put me in a place of bright light in an open peaceful place, free from all the stress and pain.

It is like what is written in Psalm 118:5: "In my anguish I cried to the Lord and He answered me by setting me free."

27.
ESCAPE FROM NAXALITE GUERILLAS

In January 2009, near the end of my first weeklong visit to persecuted Christians in a refugee camp in Kandhamal, in the eastern Indian state of Odisha, I was traveling in a van through the night in a deep jungle to catch a morning 10:00 a.m. flight from the capital city of Bhubaneswar. During my visit, I had seen homes and churches burned by fanatical groups hostile to the Christians who lived there. It was a long journey from Kandhamal, where I visited for ministry, to Bhubaneswar airport. In fact, it took nearly eight hours driving through the jungle, so we left around 2:00 a.m. We had to drive slowly through the rough unpaved jungle road to avoid rocky bumps and muddy pits.

After about an hour of driving and seeing no other vehicles or people, suddenly a dark-colored, gigantic man with long hair and a black beard, wielding a large, curved knife stepped out and pointed his weapon toward the windshield and ordered us to stop the van. The driver was startled and suddenly hit the brake to slow us down. This man with the knife resembled the story of "Rakshasas," meaning demons in the Vedas (ancient Hindu scriptures). I was sitting in the front seat with the driver, Pastor John Varghese, while the other pastors were sitting in the back seat. Having a good view of this man's face, I recognized the danger we were in. Immediately, I came to my senses and slapped the driver on his back.

"Go! Quickly!" I ordered.

He slammed on the gas, and we sped forward as quickly as we could. We watched behind us for quite a while, but no one followed us. The sudden noise and speed woke the pastors up in the back, and I explained what had just happened.

"There are guerilla groups out here," one local pastor began. "They try to hijack, rob, and kidnap people out here."

We were shocked and started thanking God for saving us from such a dangerous situation. We drove for nearly 55 km through the jungle without seeing another human being or even a village. Such scary experiences in remote jungle locations didn't stop our commitment to rebuild the lives of scattered Christian refugees.

In fact, after this miracle of God's safety and protection, we continued to help build schools, orphanages, churches, and even homes for these refugees. We have been working with these people for the last ten years, and I had the opportunity to visit the area again with my wife, Susie. While the conditions have improved, it is still a dangerous area for believers to enter and do ministry.

"Because he loves me," says the Lord, *"I will rescue him. For he acknowledges my name"* (Psalm 91:14).

28.
THE MONSOON
STOPPED IN WAYANAD

Ever since Wayanad became one of our mission fields, we regularly go to different areas around that northern Kerala region to minister to our people—mostly my cousins, our relatives, and their acquaintances and neighbors. They live in a mountainous area full of steep and winding terrain, where the climate is quite colder than that in the southern and coastal areas of Kerala.

While the climate is favorable in the southern mainland, it is quite the opposite in Wayanad, which has a very severe monsoon season. During this time, there are nonstop downpours for three to four months. In the monsoon season, very little can be done in that area as the unpaved roads become muddy and mudslides make the area very dangerous.

While driving through these areas, our vehicle frequently got stuck in the mud. One year, I was scheduled to come during this rainy season. Pastors from the area had warned me of all these climatic difficulties and potential hazards, yet, because of my time constraints, I still planned to go.

During one of my trips with a few other people, the rain was very severe. Before entering the mountainous area with the steep gradient, we prayed that the rain would stop and we would have a comfortable trip. To our surprise, when we reached the area, there was no rain. All the meetings were conducted without the weather hindering us.

After our three-day program was over, we prepared to go to another area. Manoj, a Hindu man who was also our first convert, noticed the weather and said, "Sir, you prayed for the rain to stop during your meetings, and it did not rain while we were there, but please pray so the rainfall will come back for the farmers. They need the rain."

We prayed, and the day we left, the rain started again.

Scripture References: Mark 4:35–41; Matthew 18:23; Luke 8:22–25.

29.
THE DROUGHT
IN JALNA

During my first trip to the Jalna district in Maharashtra, my wife, Susie, and I were traveling together to go visit a family member who was doing mission work there. All flights were delayed that day from Mumbai, so we had to wait almost eight hours to get a flight to Aurangabad, the nearest airport. Finally, late at night, we were able to get a flight to Aurangabad from Mumbai. When we arrived, a few of our pastors came to pick us up. It was a very hot day, about 118 degrees Fahrenheit or (47 degrees Celsius) that evening. It was also very dry. As we drove, the pastor told me there had been no rain there for the last six months. They had trucks and bullock carts on the road that brought in water to drink and for households to use.

I said, "God has no limitations! He can send rain and He can send drought."

"Yes," they replied. "We fasted and prayed and one feeble rain came, but then it just went away."

I didn't pay much attention to that. Many people of many religions prayed and did whatever they could do to please their god to get rain. They offered many kinds of sacrifices to various gods and goddesses.

We were just about to leave that night, and while we were praying, I remembered the conversation and prayed for God to send some rain to that place. We went to the city, which is about a one-and-a half-hour journey by road from Aurangabad Airport. Jalna is a Marathi speaking town with very dusty air and is congested with a lot of people, animals, and dogs. While there, we prayed for rain and then went to sleep in our small hotel room. The air conditioner was running hard to try to combat the stifling heat.

The next morning when we woke up, we noticed that the temperature had dropped. When I opened the window, I saw it was drizzling around the hotel. We didn't think much about it, but thanked God. The temperature continued to drop, and the drizzling rain continued. That morning, we were scheduled to go to twelve different villages. There were seven of us: my wife and I; the local pastor, his wife, and his two children; plus the driver. We were going from village to village to share the gospel, visiting some homes, holding prayer meetings, and praying for individuals. In each village, people gathered in one place so that we would pray and minister there. It was a long trip traveling by a three-wheeler auto-rickshaw, but by the end of the day we had finished our work and went to visit the family of a new believer.

They received us kindly and gave us some refreshments and water to drink. The rain continued to drizzle throughout the day and sometimes even small showers would pop up; however, as the day progressed, we started to notice there were puddles of water on the road and in the gutters. There were some birds sitting and enjoying a cool dip in the water. They were happy and having a good time, which made me feel happy. I began to see the difference in the areas with and without rain. By the time evening came, we were all drenched with water, sweat, and humidity, and the rain continued.

That evening we had another prayer meeting, so we washed up and went to the prayer meeting. We were told many of the people attending the meeting were new and we shared the Word. Many healings took place, which was a great miracle for each of those people, but the other miracle was that even after I left that town two days later, the rains continued.

Despite six months of drought, the rain that started on the first morning continued for fifteen days. Every lake, well, and reservoir filled up with water. While on the way to the airport, we stopped to see one of our friends, who was a schoolmaster. He is a Christian brother from Kerala, running a school in that area. He said, "This morning I purchased drinking water for my teachers and students for thirty-five rupees, (which was a huge amount for that time). You had rain in Jalna; when will we have it in Aurangabad?"

I said, "God is an impartial God. He loves everyone and satisfies our hearts' desires, and in due time you will also have rain."

Soon after, as we entered the town, it started raining! Everyone had plenty of rain: the crops, animals, people, and the birds were all happy once again because God sent rain into the hot, dry land. When God sends somebody for His service, He will find ways to establish His work there. Because of this miracle, we were able to establish many churches in that region for many years. How amazing and how wonderful is our God!

Better still, the story did not end there. As I said, there had been no rain for almost six months. All the lakes were dry at the bottom, the ground was cracking and there was no evidence of life or moisture in the lakes. The pastor told me that in the past the lake had overflowed with water, but it had dried up because of the drought. By faith, I had said, "Pastor, I see on our next trip that we will baptize many people in this lake." When we returned, we were able to baptize nine new believers in that lake with almost four and a half feet of water.

The offerings and prayers to false gods didn't bring what they needed. Now in the land where the living God was not known, because of His miracle working power, they started worshiping the one, true God.

Scripture Reference: 1 Kings 18:42–45.

30.
30-DAY GOVERNMENT DEPARTMENT SHUTDOWN

In the late nineties, our healthcare business was expanding, especially when we started the new hospice care program in Houston, Texas. This business was growing and expanding slowly, as it was a new concept in those days to provide care for terminally ill patients at home. I had received training in England for this practice, and I was managing and directing this business along with our other home healthcare businesses.

In those days, the regulatory agencies and the government were trying to regulate the hospice program in Texas. At the same time, I had a desire to serve God through an outreach to unsaved people in many countries who had not yet heard the gospel. We had referred to this global region as the "1040 window." Even while I was busy with full-time work and our growing business, I took time off to go for mission work in these regions. It often took lengthy periods of time away from work and business for these trips and to establish a ministry in some foreign countries. I had a deep desire to go and do such missions and ministry to the unsaved. Many times, my trips were from six weeks up to two months, for a couple of times each year.

When I returned from my trips, I could see that the effect of my absence had created many business conflicts and splits among the employees, and sometimes that created problems in the continuity of the business. During one of those years, we had an audit by the state health department, and they found many deficiencies in meeting government policies and procedures, which led to corrective actions by the state. This included frequent audits and the need to improve the performance of the agency. We were put on enforcement, withholding our funds until we completed these requirements. We tried many ways to overcome this and meet their requirements, but it got harder and harder to implement. Finally, they gave us thirty days to complete all procedural matters. We appealed and agreed to meet some of their requirements. We were supposed to give reports of improvement actions taken every week to certain officials, including their legal team. We also prayed before we sent these papers so that we could come out of this crisis.

During this time, the Texas Department of Health had their own problems. Within thirty days of the implementation hearing, the department that was supposed to monitor our program was dissolved by the state governor and was merged with another department. Nevertheless, we continued to compile the documents as per their requirements. But God heard our prayers, and they canceled the whole monitoring process, and our agency was cleared to be an efficiently working agency.

I considered this a supernatural act of God's provision and compassion for His children. Since then, our agency remained clear of all administrative deficiencies until it closed in 2015 when I retired.

WHAT IS BEYOND?

"Then Jesus came to them and said, 'All authority in heaven and on earth has been given to me. Therefore, go and make disciples of all nations, baptizing them in the name of the Father and of the Son and of the Holy Spirit and teaching them to obey everything I have commanded you. And surely, I am with you always, to the very end of the age'" (Matthew 28:18).

I have lived long enough to see first and second generations, and even some third generations, of those who have experienced great benefits from the supernatural works of our God. I have much reason to believe that healing, freedom from bondages, addictions, bad habits and strongholds, or simply experiencing the love, joy, and peace of the Lord by receiving freedom and forgiveness from sin, are blessings from God that brings a radical change in a person's life. I, too, am a recipient of this kind of freedom and have experienced immense blessings in my own life. If I looked at the blessings from God in my life, I would have considered myself as undeserving to have received so much of what I have enjoyed through my lifetime. If I begin to write about the wonderful grace and abundance of blessings God has showered upon me and my family, it would be another whole book that I would have to write.

Before I say any further, my honest thought and consideration is that my personal deliverance and salvation is still the biggest achievement I have in my life. The Bible says, "Seek first his kingdom and his righteousness, and all these things will be given to you as well" (Matthew 6:33). These may be the first words I learned and understood in the beginning of my journey as a born-again believer in Christ.

When a person comes to the knowledge of God or accepts Jesus Christ as their personal Savior, that is the first life-changing event that they may have ever experienced. Jesus Christ is different from all the other so-called gods and divine entities. They all claim to be gods and may even be shown to have some power to manifest some form of miracles or supernatural works, but they have no power to save a soul. Even after half a century of life as a believer in Christ, I still remember that first supernatural experience and how it changed the course and direction of my life.

In *Signs Wonders and Beyond*, there is a "beyond" impact from each story. Firstly, these miracles, healings, or deliverances have an immediate impact on the recipient—a sudden change in their hopeless condition. An encounter with Lord Jesus makes a huge difference, giving them a new hope, but not just the recipient, there are a host of witnesses to most of the miracles who also get an assurance of something better in the future—from darkness to light, from sorrow to joy and from weakness to strength. In some of the stories, we hear of second and third generations looking for the truth, but not in their religion but seeking a true relationship with this Savior. Most of the stories in this edition have a beyond experience mentioned.

A new work of God in a new believer's life begins with these supernatural encounters, while the others who witness this experience would also commit their life to Christ after seeing the demonstration of God's power, love, and compassion for the ones in desperation. In our experiences, we have seen that wherever there is a manifestation of God's supernatural presence and power to bring a change, the immediate benefit is the evangelization that takes place in that household, village, or region. Many come to the knowledge of God just based on one supernatural, life-transforming event. In many deep remote villages, God starts a new work and helps us set up ministry outreaches and eventually build and set up a church and a congregation of new believers. We then train, ordain, and mentor a local pastor, and we support them to continue the work in that region. Most of our ministry and mission work in those regions is through personal contact, then the Lord opens the way to further grow that ministry as more new believers are added through preaching the gospel through signs, wonders, and miracles, and they then begin witnessing for Christ.

More than joining an established organization, we look to recruit and train an individual to continue that work—someone who is willing and passionate, speaks the local language, and understands the challenges of the region. The secret of these new church plantings and outreaches in new villages or regions is how we operate by God's anointing, favor, and grace. Without His doing, none of this would be possible. Throughout the decades in ministry, we have reached hundreds of villages in India across seventeen states, with numerous spoken languages, preaching and teaching the good news of the gospel to hundreds and thousands of people. Our ministry has water baptized numerous new believers through these decades.

Despite the many differences in local culture, traditions and the serious persecutions from fundamentalists and radicals, our mission work is still progressing far and wide. We pray that this move of Holy Spirit power, with manifestations of signs, wonders, and supernatural events, will continue to even the remotest parts of the world.

AN INVITATION

I want to present you the opportunity to know the miracle-working God we talked about in this book. If you need a miracle in your life today, but do not know how to access it—it is very simple. A relationship with Jesus Christ is the door to a life that you could never have imagined. It is the doorway to a life of love, freedom, and hope. You don't have to be a victim of your past, present, or future because God is still able to perform a miracle in your life today and for whatever you may need in the future. He is all you need.

I invite you to repeat the following prayer:

Heavenly Father, I invite You to come into my life today.
Jesus Christ, I believe you are the Son of God and You died
on the cross for me. I ask You to forgive me of my sins and
help me start a new life.
I accept you as my Lord and Savior.
Thank you for loving me and for having a great
plan for my life.
I love you and trust you with my life!
In Jesus' name, amen!

Friends, if you prayed this prayer, we would love to hear from you.

Please email or write to us at:

Mathai Outreach Ministries International
PO Box 96495
Houston, Texas 77213-6495
Website: www.MathaiOutreach.com
email: contact@mathaioutreach.com

ABOUT MATHAI OUTREACH MINISTRIES

The many testimonies that you have read in this book demonstrate that when we turn even the most challenging trial or crisis over to God, He can make a miracle out of it. The passion of Mathai Outreach Ministries is to share the message of Jesus Christ, the good news of the gospel, to the lost, broken, and unreached population. To reach this goal, we have flown, driven, and walked hundreds of thousands of miles. It has taken us to remote villages where we've preached by candlelight, to the homeless and destitute on the streets, and into the houses of wealthy community leaders. In each place our goal is the same, to share the life-changing message of Jesus Christ.

We go into many remote areas that are unreached by other ministries. It is our heart's desire for everyone to commit their life to Christ and experience His love and forgiveness. There is an abundant life ahead of you when you release control and step into your calling. God is sovereign and has a great plan for your life, a life that will bring you the greatest joy and fulfillment. This call and commitment began with one generation and is continuing to the next. My family and I not only believe in this ministry, but we work in it and for it. We work our jobs to fund this important work, but the need is great. We encourage you to be a part of this ministry through your prayers and support. Your gift will help actively support all aspects of evangelism through Mathai Outreach Ministries because 100 percent of your gifts go to the native mission field.

In recent years, we have fully or partly funded construction and the planting of new church buildings in many communities across India. We have also funded repairs to church buildings or homes of believers that have faced attacks and persecution. In many communities, believers have no proper shelter or building with a proper roof to congregate for worship; even their homes are small hutments with temporary roofs and broken walls that could crumble during natural calamities.

Many Christian believers face severe persecution when they forsake their original religion. They are denied access to public water facilities and may often have to travel far distances to bring water for their household. Our ministry has fully or partly funded many projects for drilling and installing water wells with hand pumps in village communities where there are such challenges.

Many of our believer communities are agricultural farm workers or semi-skilled laborers who can't afford to send their children to school due to remote locations or transportation issues. Our ministry supports in funding teachers who provide basic education to the little young ones, besides providing foundational Biblical teaching while their parents are at work during the day.

Thousands of new and young believers have no access to getting a physical Bible and are less educated about biblical principles. We encourage these new and young believers to focus on reading, studying, and meditating on God's Word by providing physical Bibles in various languages. Our ministry also funds some enthusiastic youth who may want to go to Bible School.

For more information, visit us at our website, where you can sign-up for our newsletter that will keep you up to date on the latest news from the mission field.

Website: www.MathaiOutreach.com

Email: contact@mathaioutreach.com

ABOUT THE AUTHOR

Ipe Mathai is the founder and president of Mathai Outreach Ministries, a Christian-based, non-profit organization founded in 1996 focused on outreach, church planting, and training pastors across various regions of India. Through the ministry, he has also established Mathai Outreach New Hope Churches of India. Ipe attended the University of Houston - Clear Lake where he obtained a degree in healthcare administration in 1985. Ipe was a healthcare professional and business executive launching multiple healthcare enterprises in Houston and surrounding areas in Texas. In 1993, at the peak of his flourishing career, Ipe heard the voice of God telling him, "Go back to your people." Ipe understood this as God's call for him to go back to the people of India for ministry.

Ipe and his wife Susie have been members of Lakewood Church in Houston for over 30 years and have served there as volunteers. Seeing his commitment to the ministry for missions' outreach in India, the late Pastor John Osteen ordained Ipe as Minister of Gospel in 1998. In 2008, Ipe received certification to be a Licensed Minister by the International Congress of Churches & Ministries based in Chattanooga, Tennessee. Following his calling to missions, Ipe pursued his Doctor of Divinity from the International Seminary in Florida and graduated in 2012.

Ipe is also the author of *A Handful of Clay in the Potter's Hand*, an autobiography about his life, career and early ministry experiences.

Printed in the USA
CPSIA information can be obtained
at www.ICGtesting.com
LVHW011758291024
795102LV00013B/545

9 798893 330199